"My meeting with Jim to discuss the funeral arrangements for ~~~~~~~ is one that I will never forget. This is the part of pastoring that is inevitable, and although I don't particularly look forward to funerals, my desire is to be a strength and support to the family members left behind; however, this was not your typical funeral planning. I sat in shock as I listened to Jim explain the deception Melissa revealed to him just weeks prior to her death. A deception that he unknowingly lived under for thirty years. I can tell you as Jim's pastor that the story you are about to read is one that will give you hope. It will bring healing to your heart and remove the pain of betrayal. Jim is the real deal. He has faced the reality of what has happened and not lived in denial of it. May you find strength in these pages and God bless Jim for sharing his story to bring hope to others."

—*Pastor Mark Cowart*
Senior Pastor, Church For All Nations

"An intriguing and inspiring story of how grace and faith triumphed over deception, and forged the bonds of a loving marriage."

—*Dr. Jim Dyet*
Author and retired editor and pastor

"Jim Marr paints a modern day 'Hosea story' for his readers. Though Melissa was unbelievably dysfunctional, and at times unlovable, Jim chose to love and commit his life to her. I was struck by the thought while reading this book that . . . we are all Melissa! As humans, we are frequently driven by the fear and insecurity of 'being found out,' or being rejected, resulting in a mess of loathsome cycles of deception and hiding from our loving heavenly Father and hurting others. Jim paints a heartfelt picture on a human level of God's unfailing love and devotion for His 'woman.'"

—*Julie Ferwerda*
Author of **One Million Arrows** *and*
The Perfect Fit: Piecing Together True Love

What readers are saying:

"A moving and touching story. It's wonderful. I'm literally unable to tell you how I feel after reading it."

—Dave

"If I didn't know better, I would have thought it was a fictional account."

—Dennis

"I devoured the book! Honestly, it just kept me wanting more! What a fantastic love story it is."

—Liz

"I'm just blown away; almost struggling to find the words to describe how I feel when reading it. It is a very powerful work . . ."

—Bob

"A heart-wrenching, heart-warming story of faith, love, and accountability."

—Kate

HOPE AND A FUTURE.
JER 29:11

James SMan

It Was Out of
LOVE

A Memoir

It Was Out of
LOVE

A True Love Story of Deception, Grace, and Forgiveness

James S. Marr

WinePressPublishing
Your Book, Defined.

WinePress Publishing (PO Box 428, Enumclaw, WA 98022) functions only as book publisher. As such, the ultimate design, content, editorial accuracy, and views expressed or implied in this work are those of the author.

Unless otherwise noted, all Scriptures are taken from the *Holy Bible, New International Version*®, *NIV*®. Copyright © 1973, 1978, 1984 by Biblica, Inc.™ Used by permission of Zondervan. All rights reserved worldwide. WWW.ZONDERVAN.COM

ISBN 13: 978-1-60615-023-8
ISBN 10: 1-60615-023-5
Library of Congress Catalog Card Number: 2009935239

To Melissa

It was out of love that we shared 30 years together as husband and wife. I miss you dearly, but I know that you are now enjoying the pleasures of heaven. You gave me the opportunity to experience many aspects of love; although I fell short of God's best many times. I pray the Lord will continue to help me and the readers of this book come closer to his pure love each day we remain on this earth. This is our love story.

Contents

Acknowledgments

Above all, I thank my Lord and Savior Jesus Christ for giving me the vision for this book and enabling me to continue my journey toward the hope and a future he has promised.

Mom and Dad, you instilled in me the character and values of a simple man of God that made it possible to live this story.

My sister Pat, thank you for leading me to our Savior. Bob and Sarah, my eldest and youngest siblings—thank you for your unique gifts that have blessed and shaped my life in many ways.

My sister Sue and sister-in-law Norma—you two have been my greatest supporters and encouragers from those first draft chapters until the final product. Thanks, Norma, for the hours of phone calls over the last couple of years as you helped me see more clearly the meaning of the past and the promise of the future. Sue, you continue to be my inspiration to trust God more each day in the face of incredible trials.

Dennis, Suzan, David, Barbara, and the rest of Melissa's family, thank you for your support through the past three decades and your encouragement in allowing me to share these private experiences in such a public way for the glory of God.

To so many family members and friends who have provided encouragement, insight, critique, and some editing help along the way—you are all amazing. You kept me going when I felt like giving up. Thank you, Carole, for reminding me to give voice to Melissa. Thank you, Stan, for first telling me about Christian Writers Guild and the contest that motivated me to complete my first draft.

To each of the editors, agents, and publishers who have provided encouragement along the journey, even in the form of a rejection that helped guide me toward this final destination, thank you.

Dr. Jim Dyet, thank you for gifting me with the subtitle that captures so well the vision of this book.

Julie Ferwerda, you honored God by speaking the truth in love—even as I was in my final editing stages. You showed me where I was hesitant to speak some hard truths and helped me reveal the most important lessons of this bizarre story.

Finally, to Pastor Mark Cowart and my entire family in Christ at Church For All Nations—you provided the foundation for my healing, my writing, and this divine opportunity to "reap eternally."

CHAPTER 1

Valentine's Day

Valentine's Day is a day for romance, a day for falling in love. It's the day I declared my intent to marry a woman I'd never met face-to-face. Thirty-one years later, it's the day I began saying good-bye to the love of my life.

At 4:45 A.M. on Valentine's Day, 2007, the phone rang as I was preparing to go to work.

"Mr. Marr, this is your wife's nurse at the health care center. We found Melissa nonresponsive in her bed this morning. Which hospital do you want her taken to?"

I could feel my pulse pounding as my hands began to shake. The memories of thirty years together as husband and wife flashed through my mind. I couldn't help but fear I might be losing my wife on this day, of all days. *Was this the end of Melissa's long battle against diabetes and kidney failure? Was Melissa already in heaven, free from pain?*

Startled back into the urgency of the moment, I told the nurse the name of the hospital. This was not the time to ask for more details.

As I ended the call, my eyes welled up with tears. My mind raced as I tried to think of what to do next.

Over the last few years, with all the doctor appointments, hospitalizations, and months of home care, Melissa and I had endured many challenging situations together. But this Valentine's Day morning was more serious than anything we had experienced before. I ran to get dressed and gathered up a bag of things to take with me to the hospital. I was out the door in minutes. As I backed out of the garage, I realized I needed to talk to someone—someone who could pray for Melissa and for me. I stopped briefly in the driveway to call my parents.

"Mom?"

"Yes, Jim, what is it?" my mom asked with some apprehension in her voice.

"The nurse at the health care center called," I cried out through the tears now flowing profusely. "Melissa is nonresponsive and they are taking her to the hospital. I'm driving there now."

I ended the call and grabbed a handful of tissues to clear away the tears now blurring my vision and flowing down my face. I imagined what Melissa was going through in the health care center as the nurses and paramedics worked to save her life.

I struggled to navigate roads that were covered with an inch or two of slippery snow. This journey to the hospital was a route I knew all too well from the last few years of Melissa's treatment for declining health. I labored to process the rush of images coursing through my mind. I restrained myself from thinking the worst and called out to God for his help.

Thinking about what I was going to see when I arrived at the hospital, I questioned whether this emergency was really as serious as it appeared. *Was Melissa nonresponsive from something very serious, or was she only having one of her deep-sleep events where she couldn't be awakened and the nurses overreacted?* "Nonresponsive" was all I knew.

When I arrived at the hospital, I ran from the parking garage up to the emergency room entrance. I quickly made my way through the metal detectors and into the emergency room waiting area.

"I'm Jim Marr," I panted to the nurse behind the counter. "I'm expecting my wife Melissa to arrive by ambulance. Is she here yet?"

After searching the computer screen a few seconds, the nurse replied, "No, we don't see an entry yet for Melissa. Wait a few minutes and we'll let you know as soon as she's on the way."

I paced around the large waiting area that was quiet and virtually empty, except for one person seated across the room. I sat down for a few minutes to regain my composure. I made another phone call to update my mom on what I knew about Melissa's condition. After talking for just a few minutes and seeing no activity at the nurses' station, my mind turned again to Melissa and what had happened in recent weeks.

For the previous two-and-a-half months, my wife had been bedridden in two different hospitals and a health care center. She battled infections from diabetes and complications from kidney failure. Her diabetes-related sores had been making steady improvement in recent weeks, allowing her to be transferred just two weeks earlier from a long-term-care hospital to the sub-acute health care center. A rising fever two days ago, however, signaled the return of the infections. The doctors resumed an antibiotic regimen to combat these attacks on her body. Melissa's temperature was slightly elevated the next day, but she was able to make it to her dialysis appointment.

Today was Valentine's Day, but I had arrived at Melissa's room at the health care center the previous evening after work, with my early Valentine's Day presents in hand.

VALENTINE'S DAY EVE

I was disappointed to see Melissa's lunch tray untouched at her bedside as she slept in the clothes she had worn to dialysis that morning. It had been an extremely exhausting day at the dialysis center. She was fighting the recurrence of a fever. The nurses decided to wait until bedtime to change Melissa into her hospital gown. She slept most of the day.

Because Melissa had refused to eat lunch, I knew it would be important for me to help her eat something.

"Melissa, it's Jim. Are you awake?" I lightly shook her shoulder, trying to awaken her from a deep sleep. I repeated this several times.

Melissa's eyes flickered open. She moved her legs slightly and then grimaced from pain.

Groggily, she turned her head toward me and I recited a recurring theme of mine over these many weeks of hospitalization. "Melissa, I see you didn't eat your lunch today. You've got to eat if you expect to get better and go home."

"I wasn't hungry," she said weakly, as she strained to focus her eyes on me. She tried to adjust her headscarf that had fallen down over her eyes.

"I'll be sure to get some food into you tonight at dinner," I told her, reaching out to help straighten up the uncooperative scarf. "So, how did dialysis go today?"

"I don't remember anything special. I guess it was okay." She closed her eyes, as though exhausted from speaking those few words.

I helped Melissa eat some dinner, but still it was not the full amount of nourishment her body so desperately needed.

After dinner I announced, "Tomorrow is Valentine's Day, Melissa. I have a card and some gifts for you tonight. I won't be back to see you until tomorrow evening after work, and I didn't want you to think I forgot Valentine's Day!"

"That's nice. After that you can take me back to my room upstairs."

From experience, I was able to recognize when Melissa was digressing into an episode of dementia caused by her medications and long confinement in a hospital bed. Fortunately, she always recognized me. Sometimes, she would forget that I had visited the day before, or she would talk about some strange things she had seen in her room that day.

"No, Melissa," I assured her, "you are already in your hospital room where you will sleep tonight. Your roommate, Barbara, is here with you."

Barbara spoke from behind the curtain separating the two hospital beds. "Melissa, I'm right over here—this is your normal room that we share."

We continued the conversation a few minutes before I reminded Melissa that one of her favorite television shows, *American Idol*, was on that evening. I knew that most likely she would not have the attention span to watch the show and would fall to sleep soon after it started.

I walked over to the dresser to gather up my Valentine's Day gifts and card. "Melissa, I have a small box of chocolates for you."

"I don't want any chocolate."

I compromised. "Okay, I'll cut off a small piece so you can at least say you had some Valentine's Day chocolate."

She obliged and ate a single piece of candy while I gulped down several pieces myself. I gave her a small, red Valentine bear, and opened up her card and read it to her. I signed the card with my trademark salutation that goes back to what Melissa wrote on a picture she gave to me thirty-one years earlier:

Love, Forevah and Evah! Jim ☺

"I love you, too," she said drowsily.

Memories rushed through my mind of previous Valentine's Day celebrations, the thirtieth wedding anniversary we had recently celebrated in the hospital, and the tremendous challenges of these last couple of months of hospitalization, not to mention the last few years of a slow and gradual decline in Melissa's health. If this weren't enough to deal with emotionally, I was still reeling from Melissa's shocking revelation six weeks earlier about the deception she had maintained for thirty-one years.

Her confession initially convinced me that it was out of love she had deceived me into falling in love with her—only later would I fully comprehend the selfish motivations behind her actions. If I had known the truth from the beginning, I'm sure we never would have been married. Despite Melissa maintaining this deception—a deception I will reveal later, God had blessed our lives together and had enabled us to be a blessing to others. He helped me forgive Melissa and assure her of my deep love and commitment to our marriage.

Melissa, family, friends, our church family, and I continued to pray to God for her healing and for him to give his strength to both of us. It was a struggle to trust God as I watched Melissa go through so much in these recent years, but I knew that trust was the only thing to get us through each day.

> The LORD is good, a refuge in times of trouble. He cares for those who trust in him. (Nahum 1:7)

We began watching *American Idol* and, as I had predicted, Melissa was soon falling asleep. About the time the program ended, the nurses came around to prepare her for bedtime.

"Melissa, you need to wake up so the nurses can take your vital signs and get your clothes changed," I said. As she slowly awakened, I was preparing to take a break down the hallway while the nurses dressed her for the night.

Melissa surprisingly said, "Well, you'd better be getting home now."

This was entirely unexpected. At the conclusion of most of my daily visits, she would plead with me to stay longer or to spend the night at the hospital. Even if I extended my stay, she would still be disappointed when I eventually went home. I tried to reason with her many times about my need to get a good night's sleep at home before work the next day. This was a cycle we had maintained since Thanksgiving, when she began this long period of hospitalization. With the periodic dementia symptoms, any reasoning like this was usually fruitless. So her response this night was very unusual.

Realizing how exhausted Melissa was, I agreed it was time to go home and said, "I love you. Have a happy Valentine's Day, and I'll see you tomorrow."

"I love you too. Good night."

After a light kiss on her cheek, I gathered up my things and went home.

MELISSA ARRIVES AT THE EMERGENCY ROOM

As I reflected upon those precious memories of the night before, I was jolted back into the emergency room waiting area. *Were those the final words Melissa would ever speak to me?* Soon, I was up pacing again and praying to God for both of us.

And call upon me in the day of trouble; I will deliver you, and you will honor me. (Psalm 50:15)

Several more minutes passed with no status updates from the emergency room nurse. Since I expected the ambulance to beat me to the hospital, I wondered what was taking so long. I called the health care center and reached the charge nurse on Melissa's floor.

"This is Jim Marr. I'm waiting at the hospital for my wife, Melissa, to arrive. Is she still there?"

"Yes, the paramedics are stabilizing her and they should be leaving in a few minutes."

This was good news to me at the time, because it meant Melissa was indeed alive, although I didn't know exactly what they were doing to stabilize her. I could only imagine what might be going on based on the emergency room scenes I had seen on television or in the movies. Shortly after this call, the emergency room nurse reported that Melissa's ambulance was arriving. A few minutes later, the nurse appeared at the door to take me to where Melissa was receiving treatment.

As we approached Melissa's room, the nurse paused and asked me, "Are you ready for this? She's going to have lots of equipment hooked up, and this may be difficult for you."

I thought that it couldn't be much worse than what we'd already been through the past couple of months, and I confidently replied, "Yes, I'm ready."

The nurse pulled back the curtain, and I walked into the room to see Melissa unconscious and surrounded by several nurses and a doctor attending to her condition. The scene in front of me was overwhelming. In addition to the expected intravenous bags attached to her arms, the blood pressure monitor, the heart monitor wires, and the oxygen tube, my eyes were drawn to two things I hadn't seen before on Melissa. The first was a respirator tube in her mouth, and the second was tubes in her nose. The nurses called out instructions to each other in a calm but deliberate manner as they methodically worked to stabilize Melissa's vital signs. A nurse at the end of Melissa's bed documented each medical supply item as it was consumed.

I heard the usual beeping tones of various medical devices and the rhythmic sound of airflow from the respirator. My vision of this entire scene blurred, and as my eyes filled with tears, I bit my lip to restrain my emotions. I continued to observe the busy activity a few steps away. When I was able to get closer to her bed, I reached out to touch Melissa's shoulder and said to her, "I'm right here with you, honey."

The emergency room staff drew several vials of blood for various tests. Other technicians soon arrived with a portable chest x-ray device. Minutes turned to an hour, then another hour, and around 8:00 A.M. I went to a private waiting area to make several phone calls to family, friends, and my employer.

The lab results from the blood tests and the pictures from the chest x-rays came back to the emergency room staff. When I returned to Melissa's room, the doctor explained that my wife had suffered a cardiac arrest at the health care center, due to septic shock from the infection in her blood, urine, and lungs. He told me that Melissa would be transferred upstairs as soon as a room in the neuro-intensive care unit was readied. Only then would the hospital staff continue their assessment of her condition.

Two of Melissa's close friends arrived at the emergency room. They provided some much-needed emotional and prayer support during those initial hours of whatever it was we would be facing. We prayed to God for his healing touch and for the doctors' wisdom in treating Melissa. As we prayed for her, I wondered if she could hear us in her comatose state. I had read several testimonies where people claimed to have had a near-death experience and reported seeing what was going on around them in the emergency room. Melissa and I strongly believed in the scriptural promise that we have for eternal life beyond this earthly existence—I wondered if she was already experiencing a glimpse into her eternal home.

We live by faith, not by sight. We are confident, I say, and would prefer to be away from the body and at home with the LORD. (2 Corinthians 5:7–8)

I stood close by Melissa in the emergency room, trying to fully comprehend everything going on around me. Several mixed emotions rushed through me as I watched her lying in the bed, totally helpless, and fully dependent on the machinery now keeping her alive. I felt apprehension, but also peace, a peace in my spirit that God would be with us through everything. I am sure the shock of this surreal moment kept me detached from the full range of emotions I would experience later. I imagined what Melissa might be experiencing at that moment in her own mind and spirit. I thought again about our lives together as husband and wife and what lay ahead in the next hour, the next day.

As I faced what might be the end of my time with my dear wife in this life, I was comforted knowing that she trusted the Lord Jesus as her Savior, and that death for the Christian is not the end, but rather the beginning of our eternal life with Christ. As I yielded to that comforting thought, I was also admitting to myself that I didn't believe God would yet heal Melissa short of her glorified body in heaven. I knew I couldn't bear to see her endure more suffering in her present condition. In just the previous few months, I had learned some valuable lessons as a Christian about what someone will do out of love for another person—things about forgiveness and about trusting in God's perfect timing. Although I had prayed months earlier for God's mercy, I now realized it was none other than God's mercy that had allowed Melissa sufficient time to make her confession.

Melissa's confession of a decades-long deception to me on December 30, 2006, first resulted in brief anger and disbelief, but the Lord helped me express my sincere love and forgiveness to her. This is a true story about Melissa, about me, about the love we shared, about the mystery that I'm still trying to fully unravel, about the importance of forgiveness, and about the confidence we have in knowing that God is always working on our behalf.

> And we know that in all things God works for the good of those who love him, who have been called according to his purpose. (Romans 8:28)

I pray the very telling of this story will strengthen my readers who may be going through similar challenges now or who may be facing them in the future. I pray you will seek to find and fulfill God's purpose in your life.

CHAPTER 2

The Middle Child

How was it possible for Melissa to deceive me into falling in love with her and to maintain that deception for more than thirty years? I've asked myself this question many times since I learned the truth. Although Melissa must get credit for her creativity, I believe that my personality played a large supporting role in this amazing story. For anybody to believe the details of this account, they must first understand how I came to be the person I was when Melissa and I fell in love.

I was born James Stuart Marr, the middle child in a family of five children in St. Louis, Missouri. Although born in St. Louis to Stuart and Gloria in 1956, the majority of my childhood was in North St. Louis County, in the city of Florissant, where I received all my schooling from kindergarten through high school. My older brother, Bob, led the way, followed by my sister Pat. After me were my other sisters, Sue and Sarah. All five of us were separated by about three years each. As children, we had the excitement of seeing our new home in Florissant built and initially surrounded by what resembled an endless playground of undeveloped land. Over the following months and years, we watched as our subdivision grew and our playground became the neighborhood that formed the backdrop for our lives.

According to various child development studies, the middle child typically exhibits traits that are attributed to the unique relationships formed with their siblings and parents, based on their particular placement in the family birth order. Although I do believe each of us is a unique creation of God, and more than the family environment determines the person we will become, I also believe our surroundings play an important role in our development. It is enlightening to examine some of these middle-child traits in comparison with my own personality. Some studies indicate that the middle child often has a negative impression of his or her situation in life. In my case, I don't have such a negative impression of my life situation. On the contrary, as I reflect on the events of my childhood from the wisdom of more than fifty years now, I believe I have been very blessed.

Being stuck in the middle often causes children to become skilled at compromise and getting along with others. Also, middle-born children tend to adapt easily to any situation and sometimes play the role of a mediator. They prefer compromise to conflict. These traits do seem to apply to how I perceive my own personality. Although I am one who likes maintaining routines, when change inevitably comes, I can quickly adapt to the new situation and establish new routines. Avoiding conflict and trying to be a peacemaker are also traits I believe others see in me. Many of these middle-child traits played a significant role in the decisions I made later on in my life when I met Melissa and through the thirty years we shared together in marriage. I believe these traits of compromise and avoiding conflict may be the primary reasons for deciding to marry Melissa in the first place.

From this vantage point many years later, as I think back to my relationships with my brother and sisters, the usual sibling rivalries, childhood battles, and other negative memories are hard to remember. Not because they didn't happen, but in the longer view, none of those events stand out as significant. What does stand out in my memory are a variety of simple experiences that define a family growing up together. Those experiences in a middle-class family living in the suburbs of St. Louis were experiences probably shared by many others living in a similar environment.

Despite all I shared with my brother and sisters as children, we each developed our own unique characteristics and personalities, sometimes so distinct it would make one wonder if we were from the same family. Not counting my red hair that had appeared after skipping several generations, I became the one devoted to obtaining high grades in school, although in the early years I was known to get distracted.

My first-grade report card included such comments as, "His low mark is due to his being too talkative," and "He can get silly at times; that is why he has the low mark." In second grade, "He does need to stop talking in class, as we discussed before." A pattern had formed and continued into the fourth grade: "James bubbles with enthusiasm—sometimes too much." By the fifth grade, I must have gained better control of my enthusiasm, for it was characterized as, "He has a good sense of humor."

I am not sure at what point I became motivated to do my best in my schoolwork, but as academic success appeared, I developed a great feeling of defeat when I didn't do well on a test or a school project. Although I experienced a rare spanking or two over the years, it wasn't long before I was driven to do the right thing to avoid punishment. It didn't take much, as a child, to bring me to tears or cause me to become emotional about something troubling me. As a result, Mom or Dad merely had to look cross-eyed at me, and that feeling of displeasing my parents was all the motivation I needed to straighten up.

HOCKEY AND THE AIR FORCE

When the St. Louis Blues hockey team came to town in the 1960s and youth hockey experienced a tremendous growth spurt, my friends and I became hooked. We played informal garage hockey games using brooms for hockey sticks and a large cork for a puck. This led to hours of tennis court hockey in our shoes, long before the days of roller blades.

We made the transition to ice hockey in local community leagues when I was in junior high school—around 1969. Hockey became a big part of our lives, and by the last two years of high school, it had become a significant high school club sport in the St. Louis area—with full schedule competition among several of the high schools. Our crowning achievement in 1974, as I graduated from high school, was being declared "Co-Champs Mid-States Club Northern Division," with a record of 18-4-2.

As my love for hockey was increasing during high school, I also cultivated a strong desire for military service. My father had served in World War II, but that was long before I was born, so I'm not sure when or how my desire for military experience was birthed. I learned about the service academies and decided to seek an appointment to the Air Force Academy in Colorado Springs, Colorado.

My academic and extracurricular record was competitive for such a goal, so I took the college placement test and submitted my Air Force Academy application package. After completing the physical exam, I waited to hear the results of my application. Unfortunately, my childhood history of migraine headaches became a reason for medical disqualification from the Air Force Academy selection process. I later received a letter saying I had an alternate appointment to the Academy from one of my Missouri senators. Whether or not I would have been selected to attend with a full appointment, had I been medically qualified, is something I'll never know.

This news was devastating, but I used my adaptability as the middle child and reset my sights on enlisting in the Air Force. Although my academic record had positioned me well for going directly into college, I knew that my parents were not able to pay for a college education. I decided to enlist in the service and seek other college and commissioning opportunities while on active duty. Reacting to my decision to enter the Air Force instead of college, a fellow classmate wrote this note in my yearbook: "I was kind of shocked and still am about you going into the Air Force. I always pictured you as the college type with a really good stable job and everything going for you. I know you'll still get it while in the Force." Despite this classmate's shock at my change in career path, her final words would later be fulfilled in my Air Force career.

Fortunately, the infrequent headaches were not a disqualification for enlisting in the new volunteer Air Force. I adjusted my plans and prepared for this new direction in my life after high school graduation. Although I had adapted my goals, the news about the Academy medical board decision ranked as one of the most distressing times in my years growing up.

MOM'S ILLNESS

An even more serious incident, one that affected our entire family for many years to come, happened when mom crashed our car head-on into a large pillar supporting a highway bridge. It was a miracle she survived, especially when we saw how the front of the car wrapped around the pillar, and the engine lay in the front seat. She had been wearing a seat belt, which seemed unusual, because this incident became the first of five suicide attempts over the next two decades, resulting from my mother's battle with bipolar disorder.

We spent many days visiting her in the intensive care facility at the hospital and enduring the slow recovery that followed. My dad, brother, sisters, and I tried to understand what would have caused her to do this. I harbored some intense anger, I guess selfishly, for what she had done to our family. I didn't fully understand the sickness she was facing. I stood alone in my basement bedroom and yelled under my breath any four-letter word I could think of to express my rage. Although she needed professional medical as well as spiritual help, I was upset that she had actually conceived doing such a stupid thing. Her healing process was very slow, but within weeks my mother recovered from the physical injuries. The healing of the underlying bipolar disorder, however, would take much longer in the years to come.

Despite a twenty-year battle with bipolar disorder, mom was the one who guided the family on a spiritual journey. She was also the one more likely to say "I love you" in words and actions. Dad was less expressive of his affection verbally when we were growing up, but now I realize how much love he was demonstrating in everything he did. One of these less visible expressions of love that was an inspiration to me was his strong work ethic to provide for our family. He worked as a meteorologist for a private weather corporation for forty-five years, virtually all of that time on the night shift in downtown St. Louis. I see more clearly now how similar I am to him in many ways, and I have learned that the way we express our love to someone is not always visible to those who are not close to us—but it is just as meaningful.

GROWING UP IN CHURCH

My first memory of going to church was attending a Presbyterian congregation in St. Louis, where we lived before moving to the suburbs. Later, we continued attending a church of the same denomination in the Florissant area. One day my parents talked about attending a church of another denomination, and so before long we joined St. Barnabas Episcopal Church.

I followed in my brother's footsteps by serving as a helper to the church minister, and I became quite experienced at performing that role in the church services. We lit the candles, participated in the procession up to the altar area with crosses and flags, and assisted the ministers in various ceremonial duties during the services. A key difference between our previous church experience and that of the new church, at least at that time, was that the Episcopalians used real wine during communion. I always joke about this point, although the fact is that my only drinking of alcohol was done in church.

Unfortunately, my church experiences never included a personal relationship with Jesus Christ. I had limited knowledge of God gained through Sunday school classes, church confirmation, and short Bible story readings that our family would share together at home. But the God-knowledge was only in my head, and not deep in my heart. This partial understanding enabled me to have a theological argument with myself one day when I was walking home from a friend's house. I was contemplating God's omniscience and omnipresence.

I wondered, *I'm walking in this direction and I'm thinking about turning to the left, but what if I suddenly turn to the right? Hmmm, would God have known I was going to change my mind?*

This is the sort of question I would put to myself. Despite this early concept of God's presence around me, and despite being the good kid who attends church, stays out of trouble, and excels in school, I later came to realize that I was as lost as the worst sinner. It didn't take long for God to lead me to the truth, but first, high school graduation, Air Force basic training, and electronics technical school.

OFF TO THE AIR FORCE

Less than three weeks after high school graduation, I was flying to San Antonio, Texas, for basic training at Lackland Air Force Base. After a late and casual meal at the chow hall, our group of new recruits was suddenly shocked into the reality of what basic training was all about. It began with our first formation that night in the dark as we heard the ominous click-click-click sound of the approaching training instructor's large combat boot heel taps. Six weeks and plenty of sweat, blisters, and hard work later, I graduated from basic training as an Airman First Class—a promotion gained by enlisting for six years instead of the usual four. My next stop was a thirty-five-week electronics technical school at Keesler Air Force Base in Biloxi, Mississippi.

During tech school, I got involved in the Episcopal church group at the base chapel. I was asked to read a Scripture at a future Sunday service, and that led me to purchase my first Bible. That I didn't already own a Bible illustrates that something was missing in my church life growing up. Among other things, I had a serious lack of firsthand experience with God's Word. I purchased a small, black, leather-covered Bible on February 16, 1975, and from the faint pencil marks at the beginning and end of the verses, I still can find the Scriptures in the book of Romans I read for that service. "Therefore, just as sin entered the world through one man, and death through sin, and in this way death came to all men, because all sinned . . . For just as through the disobedience of the one man the many were made sinners, so also through the obedience of the one man the many will be made righteous" (Rom. 5:12,19).

As I read that Scripture, I learned that it was talking about Jesus as that obedient One through whom we would all be made righteous. That essential message, however, hadn't yet reached down into my heart—but I was getting closer to the truth.

Although I hadn't yet accepted Jesus as my Savior, God continued to bless my academic ability in tech school. I was scoring extremely well on my coursework toward becoming a flight facilities equipment repairman. In the meantime, God was gracious with me as I went through a phase in my late teen years in the Air Force. Among the dozens of films I viewed at Keesler for a mere fifty cents each, there was a particular movie that several of us airmen saw multiple times.

> Therefore, just as sin entered the world through one man, and death through sin, and in this way death came to all men, because all sinned . . . For just as through the disobedience of the one man the many were made sinners, so also through the obedience of the one man the many will be made righteous. (Romans 5:12,19)

The movie title was *Sisters*, starring Margot Kidder, the beautiful young actress who years later would play the role of Lois Lane in the Superman movies. This rather intriguing horror-suspense film about two separated conjoined-twin sisters led to what I guess should be termed an obsession or intense crush on Margot Kidder for the last several weeks of my training in Biloxi. While most of the guys who attended the film with me only imagined what it might be like to meet an actress like Margot Kidder, I decided to take some action. I began a weekly letter writing campaign to see if I could communicate with the actress and get a reply. I am sure she never saw any of those letters, though I sent them by registered mail for several weeks.

On April 1 (no fooling), 1975, I was an honor graduate of my eight-month course of electronics training, and now I was ready to travel to my first assignment. People talk of joining the military and seeing the world, but my first Air Force assignment was more like seeing the world with training wheels. I was assigned a mere 250 miles away from home on the western edge of Missouri, south of Kansas City, at Richards-Gebaur Air Force Base. On the way to my first assignment, I returned home to the St. Louis area for several weeks of military leave.

Those days at home became the most important ones I ever shared with my older sister Pat. In weeks prior to my tech school graduation, I had been receiving letters from Pat about some unusual church she was attending. I didn't fully grasp what was going on until I arrived back in Florissant, where Pat was armed and ready with a fistful of gospel tracts. One key Scripture verse in those tracts described how God sacrificed his own Son to give us eternal life: "For God so loved the world that he gave his one and only Son, that whoever believes in him shall not perish but have eternal life" (John 3:16).

> For God so loved the world that he gave his one and only Son, that whoever believes in him shall not perish but have eternal life. (John 3:16)

ACCEPTING CHRIST AS SAVIOR

That Scripture, and many others, began to sink into my spirit. After a few days of intense brother and sister discussions—or as Pat characterized years later, as brother and sister arguments—I accepted the Lord Jesus Christ as my Savior. For me, it took place in the privacy of my own bedroom when I prayed a prayer

I found printed inside one of those tracts. I wrote it out on the back of a business card, signed and dated it April 5, 1975. The card read, "Lord, be merciful to me—a lost sinner. Forgive me Lord! My only hope is placed in Jesus Christ who died for me. Possess my heart and reign there supreme. Lead me by your Holy Spirit that I may know your will in all things. My Lord! My Savior! My God! James S. Marr"

A week later, Pat and I were on a hastily arranged vacation trip to California before I headed off to my Air Force duty. This trip was the encore of our adventure in Los Angeles a couple years earlier, when I was sixteen and Pat was eighteen. On that trip, we had seen several television show tapings and the usual tourist sites. This time, we were two years older and had a different perspective as new Christians, but we still took in the sights of Hollywood as we had done before. One night we followed Patty Duke and John Astin for several blocks in the car after a show taping at a television studio. As part of my continuing Margot Kidder obsession, I had obtained the home address for the author of a book featuring Miss Kidder in the movie version, and I marked the location of that address on my map prior to our trip. Surprising to me, as we tailed Patty Duke, I could see on my road map that we were approaching that author's address.

I told Pat to take a particular turn that brought us right past the address for the author. It turned out to be a home address in a residential area, and that was as close as I ever got to anybody connected with my dream girl, Margot Kidder. On the day of our departure and on the way to the Los Angeles airport, I was amazed when I looked up to see a tall building with large address numbers matching the address I had been sending all those weekly letters to Margot Kidder's publicist during tech school in Mississippi.

The most notable event of that trip was when Pat and I met the actor Dean Jones, of Disney movie fame, after the taping of a game show pilot. My sister first caught a glimpse of Dean coming out of the actors' entrance.

"Hey, Jim, look—there's Dean Jones," my sister exclaimed as she began digging in her purse for something. "The way he talked on the game show, I think he might be a Christian. I'm going to give him one of these 'God Bless You' bookmarks." Pat successfully retrieved one of the colorful bookmarks from her purse and walked toward the handful of persons surrounding the actor.

"Sure, that's a great idea," I agreed, as I quickly caught up with Pat, who now seemed to be on a mission. "He didn't seem to appreciate those off-color remarks of the celebrities on the game show, did he?"

Pat boldly approached the dwindling collection of fans around Dean, and awaited an opportunity to present her simple gift. "Mr. Jones, I want to give you this 'God Bless You' bookmark. My brother and I really enjoyed watching the taping of your game show today."

"Well, that's very nice. Thank you. Say, if you don't already have a church to attend tomorrow morning, I'd like to invite you to visit our church in Van Nuys."

Pat and I quickly agreed with his suggestion. We attended Jack Hayford's Foursquare Gospel Church on the Way in Van Nuys the next morning. After the service, we had another brief opportunity to talk with Mr. Jones.

"Good morning, Mr. Jones. I'm Pat, and this is my brother Jim. We talked to you a few minutes outside the studio yesterday."

"Yes, of course. I'm so glad you decided to visit our church this morning."

"We enjoyed the music today and the worship service. This is a great church," I added.

"What did you really think of the game show taping yesterday?" Dean asked. "I'm sure you noticed some of that 'blue material' from a few of the celebrity contestants."

Pat responded slowly, "Well, yes, Jim and I were wondering about that also. We could tell that you weren't too comfortable with everything they were saying."

Both Pat and I sensed the struggle he was experiencing, and which I know about much better now. It is the striving to live in the world while not being a part of the world.

That experience with the Church on the Way later guided me to a similar church at my first Air Force assignment back in Missouri.

> I have given them your word and the world has hated them, for they are not of the world any more than I am of the world.
> (John 17:14)

CHAPTER 3

Searching for Love

After saying good-bye to my family in St. Louis, I stepped onto
a bus for my short trip across the state of Missouri to Richards-
Gebaur Air Force Base—more affectionately known as "Dickie
Goober." The bus stopped in the small town of Belton, right
outside the base. Grabbing my bag, I stepped down onto the
cracked concrete sidewalk and looked up to see a diner called
something like "Chicken-in-a-Basket." It was a small, weath-
ered building next to the bus stop. The driver pulled out the
rest of my luggage from under the bus, and drove away, leaving
me in a cloud of dust.

This is it? I asked myself, as I started to look for a pay phone.
My sponsor arrived to pick me up at the bus stop, and he helped
me sign into the communications squadron and get settled
into my dorm room. Within a short time, I was busy meeting
co-workers, continuing to improve my technical skills through
on-the-job training, and growing into my young career in the
Air Force.

BEGINNING MY AIR FORCE CAREER

As I devoted myself to becoming a proficient electronics technician and prepared for future growth in the Air Force, I also spent
time in off-duty activities. To grow in my newly found faith as
a Christian, I sought out a church in the local community.
Because my sister Pat and I were blessed by the church we had
visited in California, I began attending a Foursquare Gospel
Assembly in the Kansas City area. That spiritual connection
provided me a foundation for growing as a Christian and for
making additional friends outside the military environment.

One couple that befriended me and helped me get firmly
grounded as a Christian was Andy and Becky. Through their
friendship, the local church activities, and my periodic connection with my family's church back in St. Louis, I was continuing
to grow spiritually in the Lord. As I gradually matured in the
faith, the Holy Spirit showed me step by step which areas of
my life needed to change next, and I struggled to make those
changes with God's help. Although focused on my success in
the Air Force, I learned that I should first be a Christian who
just happened to be in the Air Force, versus an airman who just happened to be a Christian.

Repent and be baptized, every one of you, in the name of Jesus Christ for the forgiveness of your sins. And you will receive the gift of the Holy Spirit. (Acts 2:38)

BAPTISM IN WATER AND THE HOLY SPIRIT

When I was at home in St. Louis for Christmas in 1975, my sisters and I visited a church where the pastor was preparing to baptize people in water at the end of the service. I hadn't been baptized as an adult, so I took advantage of this opportunity once I realized the church provided a change of clothes for individuals like me who came unprepared. I was water baptized the night of December 27, 1975.

Several months later, the Lord led me to experience the gift of speaking in tongues, a spiritual gift that the apostle Paul speaks about in 1 Corinthians 12–14. Speaking in tongues is a prayer language that, when properly applied according to the Scriptures, will edify and bless the fellowship of believers in Christ.

My first experience with speaking in tongues took place at my Foursquare Gospel Church in Kansas City. I went forward for prayer in the morning service, but I didn't receive the gift at that moment. After an afternoon of praying and discussing the relevant Scriptures with Andy and Becky at their home, I returned to church for the Sunday evening service. At the end of that service, Andy prayed with me, and I was blessed with this gift of speaking in other tongues. This experience gave me another opportunity for growth in my Christian walk—just as each Christian is blessed with one gift or another to strengthen the body of believers. I wasn't any better than any other Christian, or "more saved" than I was before, but I was empowered to grow closer to the Lord as I became more faithful to live according to his teachings in the Bible.

> All of them were filled with the Holy Spirit and began to speak in other tongues as the Spirit enabled them. (Acts 2:4)

> In the same way, the Spirit helps us in our weakness. We do not know what we ought to pray for, but the Spirit himself intercedes for us with groans that words cannot express.
> (Romans 8:26)

During this time of my early growth as a Christian, God gave me a strong desire to read through the entire Bible. I started at the beginning of the Old Testament and kept reading all the way through to the end of the New Testament. This is not necessarily the recommended approach for a new Christian, but it is a habit I continue to this day. I started this practice by reading at an extremely fast pace, because I had much new territory to cover. With the same Bible I'd bought during tech school in Biloxi, and with a blue highlighter in hand, I went to work consuming page after page and marking up all the verses that stood out to me.

During this time, I soon became convicted of my Margot Kidder phase, and I decided I should turn that connection into something for eternal benefit. So I set out again on my letter-writing campaign, only this time I sent a series of letters containing gospel tracts and my own words talking to Margot about my new life in Christ. As each letter was sent, I prayed that someone on the other end would receive some benefit from what I wrote. Eventually, I stopped sending those letters as well

> In the same way, on the outside you appear to people as righteous but on the inside you are full of hypocrisy and wickedness.
> (Matthew 23:28)

and confessed my embarrassing actions from start to finish to my sister Pat and my family. We later had some good laughs joking about the whole thing, and my family, of course, didn't think any less of me for what I had done.

STILL HOOKED ON HOCKEY

My life was fairly full with the Air Force and church, but something was missing. What was it? Ice hockey, of course. I became best friends with a fellow airman and radar technician who lived down the hall from me in the dorm. Bob was already a goalie on a local ice hockey team, and it wasn't long before we were playing on the same team.

Bob and I took turns driving to the rink. I went in my new 1975 Plymouth Duster, or Bob in his old black hearse. He had purchased the hearse from a sergeant in the dorm, and it worked out great, as we could throw our large bags of hockey equipment in the back. In addition to the ice time we got playing hockey, Bob and I frequented local skating rinks during the public skating sessions. We had fun comparing the hockey skaters with the figure skaters. Bob wrote his own "Commandments of Good Ice Skating Technique." Here is commandment number two: "If a figure skater gives you an 'Oh-you-screwed-up-my-Olympic-jump' look, just say, 'Excuse me.' That might help their impression of the hockey skater. Remember, we're all in this together!"

IS THERE A GIRLFRIEND OUT THERE FOR ME?

And now I have the Air Force, church, and ice hockey on my list. What else could possibly be missing in my life? Dare I say female companionship? Success with women was never one of my areas of expertise, as most people judge success, although there were occasional minor attempts—not counting my Margot Kidder obsession. Looking back as a Christian, I can thank God for sparing me the heartache that afflicts so many who have engaged in short-term, superficial relationships in their high school years and thereafter.

I had my share of "girlfriends" from afar throughout my school days, although most of them probably never knew I admired them. All the way back to the first grade, it was Joan. In junior high it was a girl with those shorts I actually thought were too short. And during my high school years, Pattie and Joyce still come to mind. After my one and only date, I found out from my sister Sue that she heard I didn't even kiss the girl. A year or two later, I ran into that same girl at a homecoming football game and, after that, at an alumni hockey team get-together in 1975 while in St. Louis. I didn't act on any fleeting thoughts about engaging in more than casual conversation for a few minutes during those encounters.

My friends Andy and Becky had my best interest at heart when they asked if I could give their niece a ride home from work. When her family remarked how it would be good to have me around more often, it wasn't long before I felt trapped, as if I was on a train leaving the station and I could not jump off. My well-meaning friends were trying to help me form a romantic relationship, but for some reason I wasn't feeling ready. *Was God trying to do something for me that I was rejecting?* Yet I didn't feel I was rejecting God; there just wasn't a connection at that point. As graciously as I could, I let everyone know my true feelings, but I thanked them for their Christian love and concern.

Although I wasn't attracted to a relationship that several thought was right for me, I had the opposite problem back at the base. I tried to form a friendship with a young woman named Chris. She was a fellow airman who worked in the supply room, so I welcomed any opportunity to go to the supply room to look up the part number for some item we had to order from supply.

"Hey Chris, how's it going? I've got a resistor I need to put on priority order," I announced as I entered the supply room.

"Oh, hi, Jim. Do you want me to look up the stock number for you?" Chris offered in her friendly tone.

"Sure, that would be great. Thanks. I'll start filling out the rest of the order form."

Chris sat at her desk and looked up the stock number on the microfiche viewer. I wasn't the only young airman who found Chris attractive. In fact, she was good-looking *even* in an Air Force uniform. Her brown hair was styled to be above her collar—well within the uniform regulations, but she did not look too military. The sharply creased uniform blouse showed that she took great care to present a professional but very feminine appearance.

We would have these brief conversations from time to time, and I formed some strong feelings for Chris. I even felt comfortable visiting her at the base hospital after she had a minor medical procedure. That particular situation led me to imagine what might have been going on in her life, perhaps naively, perhaps with some discernment.

I felt protective of Chris and tried to offer my help wherever I could. During my late evening shifts while no one was around, I wrote a few letters to her and left them at her desk in the supply room. In those letters, I told her about the Lord and how he could help her through whatever situation she was experiencing.

One day, she came up to our work center to perform an inspection of our supply logs. I was the only one in the office at the time, so we had a good opportunity to talk privately for a few minutes.

"Jim, I really appreciate those notes you left me down in the supply room the last few weeks."

I braced myself for what I felt was coming next, but first injected, "I'm glad you read them. I'm not sure what's going on with you, but if there is anything I can do to help, please let me know. I mean that, Chris."

"Thanks for trying to help me, Jim, but there's nothing you need to do."

The message I received loud and clear from our brief conversation that day was that I should gracefully back off, and so I did. Although she didn't say anything specific in this conversation, I later learned that Chris was in a relationship with an airman at the base fire department, and so this ended my attempt at cultivating some female companionship. It was soon after this episode that I called out to God for help. In my dorm room, I knelt down in front of the desk facing the window, and earnestly prayed, *Dear God, please give me someone to love, someone to love me, and someone I can help care for and share my life.*

TELEPHONE ROMANCE

More relationship help was soon on the way in the form of a blind phone date. My hockey buddy Bob had been talking to a girl named Robbie, who worked over the state line in Kansas. Through that connection, a picture of me ended up in Robbie's hands, and then it wound up in the hands of a girl named Melissa Jo Carrington.

"Guess what, Jim? Your picture got over to this girl in Kansas," Bob announced with his trademark Cheshire cat grin. "You need to give her a call sometime."

"What did you do? So who is this girl anyway? Do you have a picture of her?"

"No, but this girl Robbie who I've been talking to says she's very nice. Her name is Melissa—Melissa Jo Carrington. You should call her."

"Oh great, you're setting me up with someone over in Kansas who is 'very nice.' Well, I guess it won't hurt to give her a call. What's her number?"

With a little apprehension, not knowing what I was getting into at the hands of my good buddy Bob, Melissa and I had our initial blind date on the telephone at the end of 1975. I made the momentous phone call shortly after my trip back home at Christmas. I was working a late shift that night in our work center on base. To get some privacy for this so-called date, I walked over to the squadron building across the street to use a telephone in the empty offices. Melissa and I didn't talk very long, and we didn't share many details about ourselves, but we made a pact to tell our friends we had decided to get married—just to give them a hard time for trying to set us up. In this unsent greeting card from Melissa, which I found for the first time more than thirty-one years after it was written, I have some insight into what she thought about our first conversation:

January 2, 1976

> Happy New Year, and I definitely hope it will be a good year for you. I suppose my sweet friends told you what I thought of your picture. Well, sometimes we do silly things incapable of reasoning. But I do think you're a very good-looking guy, and from our short conversation and what Robbie thinks of you, you are a very sweet and gentle person. You really are super! I hope someday I can meet ya.

This initial, brief telephone call was the beginning of many calls, cards, and letters as we learned more about each other. I even got a telephone installed in my dorm room to avoid the waiting line at the hallway pay phone. Fortunately, the call was not long distance from Missouri to Kansas, where Melissa lived.

Melissa and I didn't immediately set up a face-to-face meeting, but when we first started talking about getting together, she revealed that she had mononucleosis and we would have to delay seeing each other until she had recovered. Despite this obstacle, we continued talking on the phone, and were both falling in love with each other in a very short time. One day, while standing in the pro shop of a local skating rink, I experienced thinking for the first time without ever having met her personally that I loved Melissa.

Somewhere in this process of falling in love remotely, Melissa eventually sent me her pictures. She had already told me jokingly that she was the older woman, at only three months older than my age of nineteen, but up to this point, I actually didn't know what she looked like. When I placed my eyes on those photographs for the first time, I knew for certain that previous reports of Melissa being "very nice" were definitely understated. She sent a couple different photos showing her beautiful, long brown hair flowing down over her shoulders, and she had a beautiful face and smile to match. She was wearing a blouse with a flowered print over her young, thin build as she posed standing behind a chair in one shot, and in a closer head-and-shoulders pose in the other shot. On one of the photographs, Melissa had written the following dedication: *My Jim, I'll love you forevah, Missy.*

In February 1976, I was headed back to Keesler Air Force Base to attend four weeks of additional Air Force training on some new electronics equipment. By this time, I was already beginning to believe that someday I would marry Melissa. I kept a larger, framed picture of her at my bedside table in the school dorm room, and I told my roommate that although Melissa and I had never met face-to-face, I strongly believed we would be married someday. He was an older man, and married, so he provided some skeptical but wise advice in the matter. I was so convinced of my belief, however, that I wrote the following note to Melissa and sealed it up for a later date:

February 14, 1976

> Today is Valentine's Day, 1976. I am writing this note for the future. I don't know what the future holds for us, and at the time I am writing this, our lips have not yet touched. But I can say, based on my feelings toward you now, that if I ever get married, I want it to be with you. If I have given you this card to read, then you know it is true. I love you today, tomorrow, and "forevah."

Falling in love with someone while trying to keep up with school assignments and follow Dorothy Hamill's Olympic gold medal figure skating success on television does have some drawbacks. Contrary to my usual "A" work in academic settings, I was slipping down to lower scores in the "B" range. No awards adorn my wall from that training course.

LEARNING ABOUT MELISSA

In addition to the photographs I had of Melissa, from our long phone conversations and piles of cards and letters, I was forming a mental picture of her as a person. Melissa was born in Meridian, Mississippi, on December 6, 1955, to Paul and Josephine Carrington. She spent much of her later school years growing up with her grandparents on their farm in Chalmette, Louisiana.

"Where in Louisiana did you say you grew up?" I asked Melissa. "Was it near New Orleeens?"

"I grew up in Chalmette, on my grandparents' farm. It's twelve miles south of Nawlins."

"Nawlins?"

"Yes, it's *Nawlins*, not *New Orleeens*. You sound like a northerner."

Melissa's father was in the Navy and moved around frequently, which was why she had more stability with her grandparents. By this time in 1976, her father had reached the rank of Rear Admiral, so the military was one thing she and I had in common. She was a military brat, and I was on active duty.

Melissa occasionally talked with a slight southern accent. She said that she had worked very hard to unlearn that accent after moving to Kansas to live with one of her brothers and his family. She had recently completed her nursing degree at Louisiana State University and moved up north to take on her first nursing position.

Melissa attended Catholic schools as a child. Because they compressed some of the grades together, she was able to graduate from high school at age fifteen, and then later from college at nineteen years of age. She grew up with eleven brothers, the eight oldest being adopted. Tragically, the three youngest were all killed in a car wreck as a result of their drinking and drug use. Melissa later told me of a similar tragedy in her life when her boyfriend, Terry, was killed in a car accident, even sending me pictures of them together in better times.

Although her mother was Catholic and raising Melissa in the Catholic faith, her father was Jewish. One day when it was time to cook up the family pig, Rosemary, for a meal, Melissa announced to her father that they were eating the pig for dinner that night and that he would have to find something else to eat. She told of another story about one of the family goats that loved to jump on top of her father's Navy staff car and stomp all over the roof.

With a military background in common, Melissa and I would talk about her father's Navy career as an officer. As a Senior Airman in the Air Force, I, of course, thought it would be exciting to meet her father some day. She talked about her family's good friendship with Navy Admiral Jeremiah Denton, who was very well known for his experience as a prisoner of war for more than seven years in Vietnam. Admiral Denton was the first person to exit that first plane full of POWs returning to Clark Air Force Base, Philippines, in February 1973.

Melissa said her father was a lawyer in the Navy and investigated various incidents, such as when a sidewinder missile would get loose on an aircraft carrier. Her mother loved all the perks of being an admiral's wife, but her father was more down to earth. He kept a tight rein on the kids as best he could while traveling away from home much of the time. For example, he told the kids that he didn't want to find out they had gone up to New Orleans for the Mardi Gras parades, and he meant it.

After learning of Melissa's southern heritage, I often teased her about my recurring vision of her sitting on the porch and sipping mint juleps. She had taken some finishing school courses while she was growing up, and these courses taught her the proper etiquette for social situations in the fine southern traditions. I had a hard time getting images of hoop skirts and southern plantations out of my mind when she talked about growing up in the south. Although not common in that part of the country at the time, Melissa also told me she had done some competitive figure skating in her childhood. So the ice was another thing we had in common.

Melissa learned to drive down on the farm in Chalmette, so she didn't have a good background in the driving skills needed for the big city. Her father bought her a Corvette as a college graduation gift, and as a result, she became very familiar with the highway patrolmen on her way to the hospital while working as a nurse in Kansas.

"So, how many tickets did you get from the patrolmen?" I asked Melissa incredulously.

"Oh, I don't remember, it was a bunch. I think they were trying to get me out on a date."

"Oh, gosh, that's crazy. Do you still have the Corvette?"

"No, I rolled it and the stupid steering wheel knocked out my teeth."

"What, you mean you don't have any teeth?" I couldn't help but start laughing out loud.

"No, I have teeth, but the hospital had to cement them back in my mouth. I also had my gall bladder removed after that accident."

"Oh, my, Melissa, you are too much. I can hardly believe all this stuff."

As if this weren't enough, she lost her license and was dependent on other family and friends for rides to work. Having rolled her Corvette and experiencing some other accidents over the years, Melissa wasn't interested in ever getting behind the wheel again.

One of Melissa's brothers had three children, Dennis, Suzan, and David. Due to some family problems that she didn't share in detail, the three children ended up moving in with Melissa's brother Ray and his wife, Carolyn, in Lenexa, Kansas. Melissa said she was very close to her nephews and niece and helped raise them as if they were her own children, even though they ranged in ages from only three to six years younger than Melissa. Although I didn't ask too many questions about this sensitive situation, I assumed she had also spent much time with them earlier in life down in Louisiana.

Melissa started and ended her nursing career in the emergency room at a hospital in Olathe, Kansas. She had only gone to nursing school to please her parents, and apparently the reality of the emergency room became too much to handle. She told some amazing stories of life at the hospital, including one about this doctor who used scalpels or clamps during surgery and then would throw the blood-covered tools across the operating room. This doctor wasn't known for his good bedside manner. Once Melissa decided to give up nursing, she transitioned into a job working in the credit processing department at a Montgomery Ward in Kansas. At this new job, she met her friend Robbie, who would play a key role in the two of us eventually getting together.

CHAPTER 4

Looks Like True Love

During my month-long training at Keesler in February of 1976, I took some time to reacquaint myself with the local Biloxi area. While walking around the main street of downtown Biloxi, I came across a Christian bookstore, where I found an unusual book titled simply *Sex*. The book was published by a Christian house in 1969 and it had a fascinating presentation of beatnik-style themes on the topic of keeping sex within the context of committed marriage. I had annotated many pages of the book with notes to Melissa before I mailed it to her.

On the back inside cover, this is what I wrote: "Yes, Missy— This is the beginning of us—you and me forevah and evah. I have great faith in Jesus and our relationship. I know it will work. We will make it work with the guidance of our Lord. Years from now, we will look upon these first few months with fond memories. As they say: 'Today is the first day of the rest of our lives.' I want to spend it with you, baby. Forevah and evah. I Love You! Jim."

These were some very emotionally committed words I wrote to a woman whom I had never met in person. They were strong words, indeed, but that was exactly what I believed in my heart.

They became the setting for the upcoming weeks of further delays in meeting Melissa after I returned to Dickie Goober.

EQUALLY YOKED?

After I returned from my month-long training course at Keesler, the phone calls and writing correspondence continued with Melissa, and the impatience to get together intensified. While the mono kept us physically apart during this period, we had the time to discuss the Christian faith and the need for us to be equally yoked as fellow believers in Christ.

> Do not be yoked together with unbelievers. For what do righteousness and wickedness have in common? Or what fellowship can light have with darkness?
> (2 Corinthians 6:14)

Despite the strong faith testimony I wrote from Keesler, I wasn't sure about Melissa's own faith at that time. I know she was raised a Catholic, but I didn't know if she had accepted the Lord as her Savior. I knew from my own church experiences growing up that being in a church doesn't make one a Christian any more than being in a garage makes one a mechanic. As a young Christian, I had apparently allowed my emotions to get ahead of the importance that we should both be of like mind before ever getting married. We had at least one conversation that included a question from Melissa such as, "How will you know if I'm good enough for us to get married?"

On April 11, 1976, I shared my excitement with Melissa over the phone. I had just returned to my dorm room after speaking in other tongues for the first time at the Foursquare Gospel Church with my friends Andy and Becky. After describing that experience to Melissa, I sensed a growing separation between my development as a Christian and Melissa's relationship with the Lord. It wasn't long, however, before that gap would close.

Within a few weeks after those events in April, Melissa called to tell me some exciting and life-changing good news that involved a trip to see her relatives in Oklahoma.

"Jim, I have to tell you something amazing that happened this week while I was visiting family in Oklahoma," Melissa began to share.

"Oklahoma?" I asked in disbelief. "How could you go visit people in Oklahoma if I can't even come over to see you in Kansas?"

"Well, I was mainly around my family, and I thought it would be okay."

I was not deterred. "It sure seems strange that you can run all over the countryside, but you can't go a few miles to see me."

Melissa was silent on the other end a few seconds before replying, "I'm sorry, Jim, but something very important happened down there. Let me tell you everything and maybe you won't be so upset."

"Okay, I'm sorry. Go ahead. So, what happened?"

"While I was down there, I went to a Pentecostal church in Stillwater where we used to make fun of the holy rollers," Melissa excitedly explained. "I went in there to talk to the pastor when they weren't having a service and, well, I prayed with that pastor and I accepted Jesus as my Savior."

"Really? That's fantastic. Praise the Lord. I'm so glad you did that, Melissa."

"Wait, there's more. After the pastor and I prayed, he asked me if I wanted to get baptized in water. At first, I was a little scared because he wanted to do it in a small river nearby."

"A river? Was it very deep? I mean, how did you do that?"

"No, I guess it was more like a stream, but deep enough for me to go under the water. When I came up out of the water, I started speaking in tongues, you know, like you did a few weeks ago at church," Melissa said excitedly, as if seeking my validation of the whole experience.

Although I expressed my joy for this amazing experience, I couldn't help but have some doubt about all of it happening just as she had described. It wasn't the first time I had heard a testimony as remarkable as this, but the timing seemed too convenient. Just as we were dealing with concerns about being unequally matched in terms of our walk with Christ, Melissa accepted the Lord and was baptized. Although I was still skeptical, I wanted to believe Melissa and what God was able to do through her faith in him.

Growing Impatient to Meet in Person

My growing impatience with Melissa's mononucleosis sickness led to another event that raised more questions in my mind. Sometime in May or June 1976, she was talking about her nephew David's baseball games.

"David has a baseball game next weekend," Melissa declared. "You know I used to go to all his games before I got sick, and I think I might go to this next one."

Hardly believing my ears, having just a few weeks before dealt with the Oklahoma trip, I demanded another explanation. "What's going on here, Melissa? Aren't you still sick? How can you go out in public like this?"

"Well, I'm just going to sit off to the side of the baseball field, far away from the other people," Melissa said, defending herself. "Jim, you know that if we tried to get together now, it would be impossible to just sit across the room and talk to each other at a distance."

I began to see some of her logic. "Yeah, I see what you mean. After all this time, I can't imagine seeing you and not giving you at least one kiss, and I know that's off limits right now. I love you, Melissa, and I can't wait until we finally get to see each other."

"I love you too, Jim. It won't be long. The doctor says I'm almost over this stuff."

As we continued our conversation, I was able to get Melissa to mention where David's baseball game was going to be played. On the day of the game, I successfully found the baseball diamond where David's game would be. Becoming an amateur private detective with my camera and zoom lens in hand, I took several pictures at a distance, hoping to get closer to the woman I loved. Unfortunately, I couldn't risk getting too close and being discovered. I'm sure Melissa would have been furious if she had found out I was sneaking around like this. Sadly, I was unable to see her in the crowd that day—or several days later while closely examining the developed slides.

With the impatience to meet each other becoming nearly unbearable, Melissa came up with an idea to have a form of contact through another person. My parents were in town to visit me, so Melissa suggested that they and I meet with her sister-in-law, Carolyn, at a lake in Kansas. Mom, Dad, and I could at least have some conversation with a member of her family, and indirectly Melissa could have some sense of closeness with my parents and me.

Melissa gave me directions to Carolyn's house in Lenexa. As she instructed, we pulled up to the house and beeped the horn a couple times as we waited for Carolyn to emerge. Within a few seconds she was walking out the front door. Melissa's sister-in-law appeared to be at least several years older than Melissa. Carolyn had a very heavyset build, and she wore her brown hair in a short style off her shoulders. As she approached the car with a friendly, close-lipped smile on her face, I hopped out of the car to introduce myself and opened the door for her. With Carolyn in the front seat and my mom and dad in the back, we followed her directions to a small lake a few miles away. Apparently, this was the lake where Melissa spent much time with her brother's family.

As we drove around the perimeter of the lake, Carolyn pointed to a particular house in the distance, where she said Melissa was staying during our meeting. Her statement caught my attention, as I imagined Melissa peering out through a window and straining to catch a glimpse of me all the way across the lake. We had a pleasant visit with Carolyn as we sat together at a picnic table with a full view of the lake on a warm and sunny day. She was friendly and seemed to enjoy our time together, although often she acted nervous and self-conscious, frequently looking down at the table and avoiding direct eye contact. She didn't seem to speak with any particular accent that I could detect, so I assumed that she hadn't grown up in Louisiana, as the rest of Melissa's family had. Perhaps she was originally from around Missouri or Kansas when she met and married Melissa's brother Ray.

"This mono sickness has been very hard on Melissa," Carolyn shared. "She can hardly stand all this waiting to meet you in person, Jim."

"Yes, I'm sure she's told you that I've been getting very impatient myself," I acknowledged. "But if we've waited this many months already, I guess we can make it a little bit longer."

At one point in our conversation, Carolyn pulled out a couple of photographs from her purse and said, "Melissa asked me to give you these other pictures of her when she was a few years younger."

The first photo showed Melissa sitting in a lawn chair at what looked like a family picnic, perhaps when she was in her early high school years. She was wearing an all-white outfit with a sleeveless blouse, pants, and tennis shoes. Although the photo wasn't a close-up, I could see the familiar brown hair of the other pictures Melissa had previously mailed me.

"This is one of her father's favorites," Carolyn remarked as she pushed another photo to me across the picnic table.

In this second photo, Melissa looked a little older than in the previous picture, but still appeared to be high school age. She was wearing a colorful sleeveless sweater over a long-sleeved, white turtleneck blouse, with brown pants. She had a beautiful smile on her face as she sat in front of a brick fireplace. Her hair was a lighter shade than it was in the other pictures.

I thanked Carolyn for bringing the pictures and, as I exhaled a large breath of air through my pursed lips, I told her, "This doesn't make the waiting any easier, but I guess it will help me have a little more connection with Melissa."

My mom smiled and asked Carolyn, "Did Melissa give you a list of things to report back to her about Jim?"

"Yes, she's curious, wanting to know every little detail," Carolyn said, laughing.

We all had a good laugh about this unusual vicarious meeting Melissa and I were having through Carolyn. Later, I had a good conversation with Melissa over the phone about the visit, and we prayed we would soon be seeing each other in person for the first time.

Shocking News

A few days later, I received a shocking phone call from Robbie, Melissa's friend who played a key role in getting us together, as it were.

"Jim, this is Robbie, Melissa's friend?"

"Oh yes, Robbie. How are you doing?"

"I'm fine, but I need to tell you something very important."

"Okay, go ahead," I said hesitantly.

"I heard from Melissa that you and your parents were able to visit with her sister-in-law Carolyn the other day at the lake."

"Yes, that was a good idea for Melissa to set up the visit."

"Well, Jim, that wasn't Carolyn you met with. That was Melissa."

I'm not sure how long it took before I responded, but in this moment of silence, I'm sure my heart was beating as fast as my mind was racing. I tried to comprehend what Robbie had just told me, yet it made no sense. The woman we drove to the lake that day was not the same person in the pictures Melissa sent me. Carolyn, or whom I thought was Carolyn, was more than one hundred pounds heavier than the picture I had of Melissa, and it didn't even resemble her.

"What do you mean? Who is this woman in the pictures Melissa sent me?" I stuttered.

"Those are pictures of Melissa. They were taken before she had a severe reaction to some medication that caused the rapid weight gain."

Robbie went on to explain an unnamed medical condition that I soon learned was supposedly suffered by the wife of Lenny Dawson, the Kansas City Chiefs quarterback. According to Melissa, in Mrs. Dawson's case, she was able, through a newly developed procedure, to have most of this rapidly gained water weight removed shortly after the occurrence. Supposedly, she even maintained an extra set of larger clothes to wear until she could have the weight removed. The weight removal process, however, carried some potentially dangerous medical risks.

"Do you mean to tell me that Melissa made up this whole mono story to cover up this weight problem?" I asked.

"She had to do something, Jim. She'd sent you those pictures of herself when she was thinner. That was before all this happened. She was extremely upset and didn't know what to do, or how to tell you. She really loves you, Jim."

Although this revelation from Robbie explained why Melissa created the mono story to avoid seeing me in person, I was more focused at the moment on thinking about the life-changing decision ahead of me.

Robbie interrupted my thoughts. "Jim, you know you love Melissa, and because you are the good Christian you are, you can't walk away from her now."

"I know, I know, but this is quite a shock to find out the person you thought you were in love with is not that person."

"Jim, this is the same person you fell in love with," Robbie reminded me. "Would you have taken Melissa out on a date if you had first seen her as she is now?"

Facing my feelings head on, I reluctantly and embarrassingly admitted, "No, if I had met her first in person, we never would have gotten to know each other as deeply as we have because I never would have asked her out on a date."

"Well, fortunately, you got to know each other. You both love each other very much." Robbie was doing her part to convince me that this new revelation shouldn't change the relationship I had with Melissa. I suppose it is what I would have expected from Melissa's good friend.

As we reached the end of our conversation, Robbie said, "Melissa doesn't know I'm telling you this."

"Robbie, thank you for telling me the truth. I've got some serious thinking and praying ahead of me to figure out what I'm going to do."

Needless to say, I did some intense soul-searching after that upsetting phone call. I don't recall how many hours or days I kept this secret to myself, but I came to the conclusion that I could not, and would not, walk away. I don't imagine anyone would have blamed me if I had chosen to leave, but I also knew that I could not live with myself if I renounced the relationship. I felt Melissa and I at least needed some time to meet together in person and work through this predicament as best we could. At the same time, I was trying to reconcile my feelings with the facts, and trying to explain to myself what in the world had happened.

Had I fallen in love with a picture? I questioned myself.

No, I realized it was much more than a picture, as Melissa and I were sharing our hearts, our feelings, and our dreams through hours and hours of phone calls, long letters, and post-cards. And there was no denying we were also growing in love at the spiritual level, so I knew my love was based on more than my infatuation with a picture.

A battle raged in my mind and spirit as I assessed the impact of Melissa's actions. *She lied to me, she deceived me, and she tricked me. How can I continue this relationship?*

This was the ultimate bait-and-switch with extremely serious implications. While I dealt with my own feelings, I honestly tried to see Melissa's motivation out of love for me. She was trying to protect me from the "bait-and-switch" and perhaps hoping that her normal appearance would be restored before we met in person. I imagined she started down this path without thinking of the final outcome, and as her mono story dragged on longer and longer, and her predicament wasn't changing, she must have hoped it would all work out somehow.

I called Melissa and dreamed up some reason why I needed to meet briefly with Carolyn. She bought it. I drove over to Lenexa, picked up "Carolyn," and we drove to a nearby highway rest stop to have a brief conversation. We shared some initial jokes about the unusual meeting place and hoped we would be safe, as we kept an eye on a few other vehicles parked at the rest stop.

The tone got more serious when I faced her and said, "Melissa, Robbie told me the truth."

After a brief pause in total silence, Melissa began to cry. Then I began to cry. For the first time in over six months, at a rest stop in Kansas, we kissed.

CHAPTER 5

Preparing for Marriage

The amount of time I spent talking to Melissa on the phone dropped dramatically as I began spending more time driving between Missouri and Kansas to see her in person. Whenever possible, I made the thirty-five minute drive from Belton over to Lenexa. Although Melissa and I thought we knew everything we could possibly know about each other, we now had to get reacquainted face-to-face. Individual mannerisms and body language were all new things to learn about each other. Obviously, you don't pick up those things over the phone.

I had the added mental adjustment of Melissa's entirely different physical appearance from what I had seen in the pictures earlier. At the early stages of a new relationship, a small, annoying trait may be enough to push a couple apart. In our situation, however, I felt as if we were already committed to each other before we ever met, giving us no choice but to work through these adjustments.

Getting to Know Each Other All Over Again

I was back to Ray and Carolyn's house on a regular basis picking up Melissa. Although I was picking up Melissa, who was no longer pretending to be her sister-in-law, some things didn't change. I still wasn't allowed to enter her house in Lenexa. Although I believe the real Carolyn, whom I hadn't met, didn't have an issue with our relationship, Ray apparently didn't want me coming inside whenever I came by the house. I would pull into the driveway at the appointed time and wait for Melissa to see me through the window and come out to the car. She would get in and we would be off, usually to nowhere in particular.

With me living in the dorm at the base, and Melissa's house off limits, we initially didn't have anywhere to go, other than to public places. To save some driving time on the weekends, I frequently got a room at the Days Inn motel in Lenexa, my "home away from dorm" for many weekends. This gave us a place to land when I would come over to visit. It was either do this or drive around aimlessly in the car. This arrangement provided us plenty of time together in private—sometimes too much. With all that we had said to each other in our love letters over the previous six months, we now had to struggle with not getting to know each other too well physically, too soon. I would bring Melissa back to her house each night, while I'd sleep at the motel.

Eventually, Melissa had to endure my collection of 35mm slides that I had been taking ever since my days at Keesler. I decided to show her every one of the 1,500 slides I had amassed by that time, which was less than a quarter of all the slides I would have in my collection years later. I brought my slide projector and slides over to Days Inn, and we had a long night of watching what I had documented of Keesler, my family, and Dickie Goober. As far as adding Melissa to my collection of slides, it wasn't going to happen anytime soon. She insisted

I keep her out of any pictures I took when we were alone or when visiting with our friends.

Something that was very difficult to adjust to was Melissa's smoking. This she had never mentioned on the phone. For a nonsmoker like me, her habit was one more challenge I had to deal with, and ultimately another compromise I had to make in our "no turning back now" relationship. On any trips around town in the car, Melissa had to hang the cigarette out the window. I drew the line at smoking in the car, and I wanted to be sure that no ashes ever made their way into that ashtray. I never made it easy for her to smoke, from those early days of our relationship until years later when she finally quit.

Because Melissa didn't drive, I was obligated to provide transportation, but she had to be the one to purchase her cigarettes. Once when she was feeling sick, she asked me to go pick up some cigarettes at the store. My immediate response was, "If you are too sick to get out of the house to buy cigarettes, then I guess you are too sick to smoke."

ENGAGED

As these initial days and weeks went by, we continued to express our affection and love for each other, but I guess things were not moving fast enough for Melissa. Before long, I got another call from her friend Robbie. Apparently, she and Melissa had been talking about us at work or on the phone.

"Jim, with all the talk about getting married before you two met, I think Melissa is concerned you may be changing your mind."

Once again, Robbie was facilitating our relationship. Although I was annoyed by this call, I used it to put myself into action. I bought an engagement ring in downtown Belton, and I inserted that sealed Valentine's Day note I had written four months earlier into the ring case.

I now had to select a proper place where I could propose. That was a challenge since we couldn't simply go to Melissa's place or mine. In those early days, we didn't even go out to any sit-down restaurants to eat. Suddenly, it dawned on me: I knew the perfect place. It was a location we would never forget, as we occasionally went there when we had no other place to go. It was a dead-end cul-de-sac in front of Grainger Pump, a supplier for a variety of pumps and other industrial products. I picked her up on a Wednesday evening, July 14, 1976, and matter-of-factly suggested we drive over to Grainger Pump to talk.

As we pulled up to the dimly lit cul-de-sac, the significance of this moment registered in my mind. Feeling a little nervous about the question I was about to ask, the events of the previous few months raced through my head.

Am I doing this out of duty because of all the things I said before we met? Do I really love Melissa as she is now, or am I still in love with how she used to look?

Although I had some reservations, I made the decision to love Melissa, and trusted that God would help my love grow deeper in the coming months and years.

"Melissa, I love you," I said, as I began to reveal the box containing the engagement ring. "Will you marry me?" I opened the box to reveal the ring.

"Yes, Jim, I love you so much. You just don't know."

I placed the ring on her finger and as we hugged each other and sealed the moment with a kiss, I excitedly pulled the sealed note out of the ring box that I had written on the previous Valentine's Day.

"Melissa, you have to read this note. I wrote it to you back on Valentine's Day for this moment."

Melissa opened up the sealed note and read those prophetic words I wrote from Keesler that foretold this occasion. We now were engaged to be married.

As Melissa and I were getting to know each other better, the time came for me to break the news to my church. Because of the attempted relationship with Andy's and Becky's niece, it would be uncomfortable for Melissa to start going to that church, not to mention all the driving we'd have to do each week. Throughout the months of our phone relationship, I was keeping the church, and Andy and Becky, informed of what was going on. I explained the situation to my church family and told them I would be attending church with my fiancée nearer her home in Kansas. Melissa and I now had to find a church we could attend together, closer to Lenexa.

The Lord soon led us to the Full Gospel Church of Olathe, a new church formed a few miles from Lenexa. Pastor Jim and his family were originally from South Africa, so he had a strong accent that was pleasing to listen to as he preached. In those early days, I helped out with publicity for the new church by going door-to-door with other church members handing out brochures about this new ministry. I also got involved in teaching some adult Sunday school Bible lessons. Melissa enjoyed the classes I taught on the miracles of Jesus, and years later, she would fondly remember those days back in Olathe.

We made many good friends at that church who quickly became aware of our geographic challenge. They understood that I had to drive over to Kansas on weekends to pick up Melissa, attend church, and later head back to the base. One couple who became very important to us during our engagement period was Don and Barb. Don was the song leader who led us in singing upbeat worship songs as well as some of the older hymns. On the faster songs, he played along with a tambourine. We thought he must have been a Christian all his life and assumed he had a sweet spirit from the very beginning. We later learned of his less than angelic past life from which the

Lord had delivered him, a real testimony of the new creation we are in Christ when we choose to follow him.

> Therefore, if anyone is in Christ, he is a new creation; the old has gone, the new has come!
> (2 Corinthians 5:17)

It wasn't long before Don and Barb opened up their home to us in true Christian love. They lived a few blocks away from our church in Olathe, and we spent many afternoons at their home after worship. On a few occasions, I spent the weekend there. We became very good friends with their entire family, including the children and their other relatives in the area. One evening while I was house-sitting for Don and Barb, I brought Melissa over for the evening to visit. As a result of her teeth being damaged during the car accident when she rolled her Corvette, she had been experiencing chronic pain in her teeth and gums. She frequently applied some pain-relieving ointment to provide temporary relief.

The pain in her teeth bothered Melissa so much that night that we prayed together, asking the Lord to stop the pain. At the end of my prayer, I closed with the familiar phrase, "in Jesus' name," but I noticed she was not repeating the name of Jesus. It got rather strange for an hour or so as I kept trying to get her to say the name of Jesus and she couldn't. I did not believe there was a demon around every corner, but I did believe we were engaged in some serious spiritual battle that we didn't fully understand. I tried and tried, and still Melissa seemed utterly unable to say the name "Jesus." We kept praying and talking, and eventually, thankfully, she was able to speak the name of Jesus before I took her home that night.

FAITH AND HOPE

One day while we were driving around Olathe after church, Melissa asked me something out of the blue. "Do you think I should talk to the doctor about getting some of this extra weight off?"

"Do you mean by doing some exercise and changing your diet?" I asked, not really believing that was what she meant. Yet I wanted to be sure.

"No, I mean having the doctor try that procedure to remove the weight more quickly. You know, as Lenny Dawson's wife does whenever this happens to her."

"Didn't you say that procedure could be dangerous?"

"Well, yes, I've heard it can be a little risky."

I thought about the best way to answer this question that had no good answer. *If I tell her to have the risky procedure done, it will imply that I'm not happy with her the way she is. If I say she shouldn't have the procedure, she may eventually face more serious medical risks from carrying all this extra weight.*

I thought it might be too late to do anything now, so I answered, "Melissa, I think you should work on improving your health one step at a time. I don't want you to have that medical procedure."

Later that summer of 1976, my sister Pat and her good friend JoAnn drove up to Kansas City from St. Louis to visit Melissa and me. As young Christians, Pat and JoAnn were on fire for God and doing the best they knew how to do with their growing faith. They suggested that we earnestly seek God in prayer that Melissa would be healed, and the weight would come off immediately.

We spent a late night praying in faith that the Lord would move in a miraculous way by the next morning. After I dropped Melissa off at her house that night, Pat, JoAnn, and I spent more time praying and confessing the Scriptures in the

> Now faith is being sure
> of what we hope for and
> certain of what we do not
> see . . . Through Jesus,
> therefore, let us continually
> offer to God a sacrifice of
> praise—the fruit of lips that
> confess his name.
> (Hebrews 11:1, 13:15)

car before I took them back to their motel. We prayed again the next morning that when I would go pick up Melissa, she would walk out the door with the extra weight totally gone. That didn't happen.

Whether our prayers were done in faith or the presumptuous actions of immature Christians putting a timeline and a demand on God, I'm not sure. Through that incident, I stopped looking for any quick miracle to get back the earlier Melissa of the picture, and I knew I had to accept her as she stood before me. That acceptance was not an easy thing to do, and as a result, we would face many challenges through the early years of our marriage.

Melissa Cut Off from Family

When it became clear to Melissa's mother that she was leaving the Catholic Church by professing her born-again experience, Josephine issued a matriarchal edict to the rest of the family.

"Jim, my mother is upset that I'm not going to attend the Catholic Church anymore," Melissa sadly reported.

"How serious is it? What is she going to do about it?"

"She doesn't want any of my brothers or their families to have contact with us. No one is allowed to attend our wedding."

"Well, that's silly. Don't you think she's going too far?"

"Yes she is. This doesn't make sense. I can't believe that none of my family will be allowed to come to our wedding."

I thought it very strange that Melissa's mother would prevent the entire family from having anything to do with us. Expressing my anger at the whole situation, I made some insensitive remarks about the pope and Mickey Mouse. It was uncalled for, and I later asked Melissa to forgive me. What with her family seeming to be moving away from us, we needed to keep ourselves as close to each other as possible. Because of her mother's dictate, Melissa's family was now cut off from any contact with the two of us.

From time to time Melissa talked about her brothers, where they lived, and what they were doing in their lives. It was incredible that I never had the opportunity to meet any of them. She said one brother was a monk in a monastery who had taken a vow of silence. I've forgotten any details about the others.

We continued to support our church in Olathe, spend time with friends, and began making plans for our wedding. During these months of planning, Pastor Jim decided he was going to return to the original denomination in which he was first ordained, which meant he was going to take a pastorate of another church in the local area. Of course, this came as quite a shock to everyone in our church, as Pastor Jim was very close to all the members of the congregation. We visited Pastor Jim at his new church home, but we didn't feel the Lord was leading us there as Jim had been led. We soon started attending Full Faith Church of Love, in Kansas, for the remaining weeks leading up to our wedding.

WEDDING PLANS

Although we originally planned to be married at the Full Gospel Church of Olathe, now that we were attending a much larger church where we were brand-new members, we didn't know where to hold our wedding service. Don and Barb graciously offered their home for an intimate wedding setting, so we went about making plans for such a wedding to take place in the middle of January. We still wanted Pastor Jim to perform the ceremony, and thankfully he agreed.

One day as we were planning the wedding details in my motel room, Melissa was on the phone talking with her mother. Although I could only hear her side of the conversation, I could tell the topic of discussion suddenly turned more serious. As Melissa's eyes teared up, the phone call ended.

"Melissa, what's the matter? What were you just talking about with your mother?" I asked, as I handed her a tissue.

"My mother told me that she and my father adopted me, as they did for my older brothers. They aren't my real parents."

"They adopted you? She broke that news to you over the phone just now?"

"Yes, she thought I needed to know before we got married."

Melissa took the news of her adoption rather hard at first, but got through that shock in a relatively short period of time. Perhaps because she had always known that her brothers had been adopted—and she knew how much her parents loved them—she was able to accept what her mother told her. She knew this new revelation didn't change anything about the life experiences she had growing up with her family, and she never expressed any desire, at least to me, to seek out her birth parents.

Melissa and I applied for our marriage license and obtained the required blood tests. We had to produce our birth certificates and Melissa was only able to come up with a Catholic christening certificate. I guess due in part to the way in which she was adopted. This raised some serious questions in my mind about whether her adoption was even legal. Why didn't her parents already have a certified birth certificate from

Mississippi? Nevertheless, the documentation was sufficient for us to get our marriage license approved, and that was all that mattered at the moment. After we were married, though, the need to track down Melissa's official birth certificate became a point of contention that I kept bringing up many times. Because we didn't know at what point we might need such official documentation, I was insisting that she find her birth certificate as soon as possible.

During the final days of our wedding preparation, we rented an apartment near the main gate of the air base in Belton. With a small amount budgeted to buy some furniture, we tracked down everything we needed by visiting the used furniture stores and thrift shops in the area. Melissa's creative craft and homemaking skills emerged as we put together a comforting home where we would begin our lives together.

I thought Melissa must have learned her craft and decorating skills from her mother and grandmother at a young age. After all, she wouldn't have had much opportunity to learn those things during college, or since moving up to Kansas. These skills showed how talented she was in those areas, and perhaps why she really didn't want to be a nurse. She also acquired another talent in Belton when she discovered a macramé shop during our engagement. Melissa took several classes and became quite skilled at that difficult craft of tying knots in patterns. This meant I had to become highly skilled at putting hooks in the ceiling wherever we moved for the next few years. Each of our homes was plentifully adorned with hanging macramé tables and potted plants.

I Now Pronounce You

The day before our wedding ceremony brought snow and cold temperatures all around Missouri and Kansas. My brother Bob and his wife, Norma, will never forget their trip across the state of Missouri in a blinding snowstorm. They were hauling a trailer that was swaying dangerously back and forth with some heavy furniture items from my bedroom in St. Louis. Thank God, they made it safely. The same could not be said for our wedding cake, however.

Our wedding was a rather low-budget operation. Melissa and I picked up the cake from a friend in Belton who created it for us. I carefully placed the box containing the cake in the trunk of the car, thinking that if I drove carefully everything would be safe. A pair of railroad tracks somewhere between Missouri and Kansas, however, had wicked designs on that work of art. When we arrived at Don and Barb's house in Olathe, we were shocked to find that the top level of this simple three-level cake had fallen off and rolled around in the box, which was definitely some added stress neither Melissa nor I needed. My sister-in-law Norma gets the credit for saving the cake. She put it back together and smoothed out a few rough spots right before the wedding, and all was well. (Or at least no one knew the difference.) The flowers and all the other details fell right into place.

Fortunately, Melissa allowed me to take a few pictures of our cake, Pastor Jim, and Don and Barb, but not any of Melissa herself or the guests who came to our wedding. We had about fifty family and friends at this intimate wedding in Don and Barb's home. Using the technology of the day, before and after the wedding we had an eight-track tape playing the music of the group Love Song. In addition to my family and JoAnn from St. Louis, we had several friends from the former Full Gospel Church of Olathe, and several friends and co-workers from Richards-Gebaur, who joined in our celebration. Andy and Becky, as well as their pastor, also attended.

Not a single one of Melissa's family members, nor any friends who knew her before we met, were present at the wedding. I knew the reason for her family not showing up, but I don't recall what Melissa's explanation was for the fact that none of her co-workers and friends, especially Robbie, attended the wedding. For such a cold and icy night in Olathe, Kansas, it was quite warm for Pastor Jim and the wedding party as we stood right in front of the roaring fireplace. God blessed the evening, and Melissa and I were pronounced husband and wife, on January 15, 1977.

After the wedding, Melissa and I were off to our so-called honeymoon at a hotel in Kansas City. After we had a meal brought up to our room, we read some Scriptures and prayed together for God to bless our lives as a couple. Although a nicer hotel room than the one I had been occupying, it still was just a local hotel room. There was no grand honeymoon trip to a romantic location for us. Nonetheless, it was special, as it was our first opportunity to fully express our love for each other.

We originally planned to stay at this hotel for a few days, but by the next morning, we wanted to get our presents and get back to our new apartment. Much to Don's and Barb's surprise, we called to warn them we were coming by their house to pick up our wedding gifts. We were ready to get started on our lives together as husband and wife.

CHAPTER 6

Starting Our Lives Together

How do I begin to summarize thirty years of marriage? During our years of moving around with the Air Force, Melissa and I frequently gauged the progression of time by the places we lived, the Air Force assignments I had, or the various churches we attended over the years. In those terms, our marriage statistics stack up this way: seventeen different addresses, eight Air Force assignments, two civilian jobs, and at least twelve different church homes. But our marriage was much more than mere statistics; it was a time of growing more in love with each other and sharing our lives through good times and bad times, in sickness and in health.

We created many memories of having fun with family and friends, or all the times the two of us simply enjoyed being alone and watching a movie or television show together. We didn't agree all the time, but we worked through

> Share with God's people who are in need. Practice hospitality.
> (Romans 12:13)

our differences and continued building our marriage one day, one month, and one year at a time. Through all of our travels, Melissa excelled at quickly turning each apartment or house into a home, and then serving others with hospitality both in the home and through church ministries.

OUR FIRST HOME

As we settled into our first apartment in Belton, we had the initial task of finding our first church home as a married couple. We got involved in a newly formed sister church of the Full Faith Church of Love we had attended in Kansas. It was called The Shepherd's Fold, and it met in the Lions Club building in Grandview, a few miles north of Belton. I became part of the initial church board, and later served as the treasurer of this small congregation of up to one hundred persons. Melissa was a skilled organizer for various church functions and dinners, and she was a great cook who excelled more at cooking for large crowds than limiting herself to cooking for two.

From the beginning of our marriage, Melissa and I were faithful in giving our tithes, or a tenth of all our earnings, as taught in the Bible.

We also gave offerings above a tithe as the Lord led us. Melissa had some reticence about all the giving, and this reticence increased

> Bring the whole tithe into the storehouse, that there may be food in my house. Test me in this, says the Lord Almighty, and see if I will not throw open the floodgates of heaven and pour out so much blessing that you will not have room enough for it.
> (Malachi 3:10)

as my Air Force salary increased over the years. Throughout our marriage, we never compromised on the tithing. But concerning offerings, I felt we needed to be in agreement for any significant amount we contributed. As a result, we ended up somewhere in the middle. I was more inclined to give larger amounts, but as she had a better sense of discernment about certain things, I trusted God to provide wisdom to both of us through her insight.

At times, I was too easily convinced to make donations by a dramatic story that captured my emotions, or by an urgent need that had to be met. A childhood friend used to pull my leg about many things and catch me time after time for being too gullible. Melissa's balancing restraint was a blessing from the Lord in such situations. After many years of marriage, she came to realize that I couldn't be trusted answering the phone or door if someone was selling something or asking for a donation.

Concerning spiritual maturity and dedication to personal Bible reading and prayer, I knew that as the spiritual head of our household I should set the pattern for both of us. With the Lord's help, I did my best to set an example through my own actions, but I always had a difficult time getting Melissa to join in. In most of our years of marriage, after Melissa stopped working outside the home, she had plenty of time during the day for Bible reading and prayer while I was at work or out of town. But from what I could see, it usually wasn't happening. It was always a challenge when I tried to encourage her to pray with me on a regular basis and discuss passages of Scripture. When it came to significant decisions, however, Melissa would join me in prayer. At times she would even pray out loud, but in general, she wasn't outwardly expressive in these activities. I had to trust that God was reaching her spirit.

As we grew as Christians, both in the church and in our home, we continued to express our love for each other in the usual manner with greeting cards, flowers, and gifts on special occasions—or for no reason at all. We weren't ones to go overboard, and we were usually very practical, but we never failed to mark such occasions in some way, such as going out to dinner.

Melissa was definitely not one for surprise birthday parties, but it sure didn't keep her from getting me good on my twenty-first birthday, just a couple months after we were married. She made up some story about having a Tupperware party at the house and instructed me to go to the office until she called me home. When the "party" was finished, Melissa called me to say that I could now come home. I returned to a packed apartment full of friends, and a loud "Happy Birthday" greeting. I was so shocked that I dropped my briefcase and walked back out the door for a few minutes. Melissa went to a lot of trouble to pull off this surprise, which certainly was an expression of her love for me. This experience also demonstrated her unique skill for keeping a secret from me, and, not for the last time, I fell for it.

To mark our first Valentine's Day after being married, I laid out a series of colored note cards in the form of arrows leading across the bedroom carpet up to the bed. The arrows ended on the bedspread,

Husbands, love your wives, just as Christ loved the church and gave himself up for her.
(Ephesians 5:25)

May your fountain be blessed, and may you rejoice in the wife of your youth.
A loving doe, a graceful deer—may her breasts satisfy you always, may you ever be captivated by her love. Why be captivated, my son, by an adulteress? Why embrace the bosom of another man's wife?
(Proverbs 5:18–20)

where I had spelled out the words "I Love You," with those same note cards. Although I frequently fell short in expressing my love as much as I should have, I knew the high standard set by Scripture for how a husband should love his wife and be committed for a lifetime to only her.

Given our history of writing many cards and letters during our initial six-month telephone relationship, it wasn't difficult to pick up that habit again. This was something I could easily do whenever I traveled to another Air Force training class. Surprisingly, not one of those cards or letters remains. I guess we thought we should censor ourselves and get rid of the evidence. On short trips, where I wouldn't be gone long enough to send any mail, I tried to find a postcard and mail it from the airport as I was leaving town with some simple note saying, "I Love You."

I'd leave notes around the house for Melissa to find during the days of my time away from home. I enjoyed talking to her on the phone while I was out of town, and hearing about her discovering another note somewhere in the house. Once I used a delayed reaction note by writing something on the mirror that wouldn't show up until she had steamed up the bathroom by taking a shower the next morning. Eventually, with the advent of cell phones, I called Melissa on each leg of a work-related journey away from home, or whenever I made an unscheduled stop on my way home from work while in town.

When we were first married, I joined a Christian tape club and enjoyed playing music throughout the apartment. That would become a source of some debate as Melissa would often ask, "Is that the only music you are going to listen to?" Or she would say, "You'll be so heavenly minded that you won't be any earthly good." Although we had some different opinions about how we should live our lives as Christians, I trusted God to help each of us serve him according to his will. Through the years of involvement in a number of churches, Melissa was hearing the Word of God and getting involved in women's Bible studies and various prayer and fellowship groups that we hosted in our home. I knew the Lord was working in her heart. Throughout our marriage, she expressed kindness in providing words of encouragement, a listening ear, and a much-appreciated sense of humor for her family, friends, and me.

First Trip to Wyoming and Colorado

In the summer of 1978, Melissa and I planned a long vacation trip out to Wyoming and Colorado. By that time her brother Ray had moved with Dennis, Suzan, and David to Rawlins, Wyoming. Melissa never explained what happened to Carolyn, and the truth is I never met her. I believe Ray and she divorced before he moved to Rawlins with their kids. It became a common understanding in our marriage from the beginning that I shouldn't ask too many detailed questions about Melissa's family. I had learned that her mother, Josephine, who adopted her, was born in Mexico. But that was almost about all I learned. I therefore assumed there were various issues in Melissa's family that she refused to discuss.

Given that no one from Melissa's family came to our wedding, we began our marriage with absolutely no contact with her relatives. Gradually, however, through the years some family communication began and relationships slowly formed. Surprisingly, even though they were living over in Lenexa during our first year of marriage, I never met Dennis, Suzan, or David before they moved to Wyoming. It wasn't until this vacation trip that I met them for the first time. For reasons that were never clear to me, I was under strict instructions around her family to call her Charlene instead of Melissa.

I had only known Melissa as Melissa Jo Carrington. When we first learned of her adoption, there was some issue with the name her adoptive family used growing up versus the name she may have been given at birth. It was all quite confusing to me. Other than the church christening certificate we used for getting our marriage license, the only other formal documents of Melissa's that I ever saw were her social security card and her pay stubs from Montgomery Ward. Both of those documents carried the name Charlene F. Marr, after she had the last name updated.

Originally, her social security card carried the same last name as Ray and Carolyn. Melissa provided some explanation that when she moved up to Kansas to start working as a nurse, Carolyn helped her get the social security card and for some reason she had a different name on it—something about another Charlene in the family. In addition to Melissa needing to track down her official birth certificate, she now had to get the name on her social security card corrected. And I didn't let her forget. Eventually, about ten years later, she successfully got her card updated to say Melissa Jo C. Marr.

During this visit to Wyoming, we stood in the front yard of Ray's house with the kids, but I was not allowed to enter the house and I never met Ray on that trip. Melissa and I saw some spectacular mountain scenery in Wyoming and Colorado, and we had a good first visit with Dennis, Suzan, and David.

Our first stop in Colorado was at Estes Park, where we spent a couple nights in a cabin beside a trout-filled stream. We continued our journey farther south to Colorado Springs, where we visited the usual tourist spots culminating in the grand finale before heading home—the magnificent U.S. Air Force Academy. Naturally, the visit to the Academy rekindled the memories of my disappointment only a few years earlier in high school. It also inspired me to volunteer a few months later for a special-duty assignment as an enlisted technician at the Academy planetarium. I was not, however, selected. It would be many years later before my Air Force career would lead us back to Colorado to stay.

After this trip, we had a number of other key events take place in 1978. We were already in our second apartment by this time. In August of 1978 we moved once again, this time to our first on-base house. Right around that same time, I had to spend several weeks back at Keesler for a leadership school, just before my sister Pat got married. We made it to Pat's wedding in St. Louis, and this trip became a momentous occasion. The reason: after about nineteen months of marriage, Melissa agreed to have the wedding photographer take our first picture together as a couple.

Keeping with plans I envisioned when enlisting in the Air Force, I started taking night school courses at the local community college. I knew that if I was ever going to qualify for the Airman Education and Commissioning Program, I needed at least a year's worth of college credits. This program would fund the remaining three years of study followed by a three-month assignment to Officer Training School. I began my preparation with a refresher mathematics course, realizing the road ahead would be extremely long if I could only manage one class at a time. Yet, one course was all I could handle because my Air Force job required standby duty at the base. Besides, I was trying to keep up with my marriage and church activities as well. Melissa was my biggest cheerleader, encourager, and best friend. She fully supported all my efforts to advance toward my Air Force career goals.

MELISSA'S NEPHEW MOVES IN

After an already busy 1978 with our travels and moving on base, we were about to experience another noteworthy event in our young marriage. Melissa's nephew David was in his last year of high school in Rawlins, Wyoming, but he was having some problems keeping focused on getting his diploma. Melissa discussed this with her brother Ray, and they came up with the idea to have him finish high school with us in Belton, Missouri. So, David packed up his things and came to live with us in our new home at Richards-Gebaur.

We had some adjusting to do when David moved in, but we worked through the challenges of raising a teenager who was only about five or six years younger than we were. Melissa was highly motivated to see David graduate from high school, and she helped him get his school assignments completed. As a result, you can be sure she was planning to see her nephew go through the graduation ceremony and make it official. Although David was willing to bypass this formality, he knew better than to challenge his Aunt Charlene on this topic. I enjoyed taking some classic photos of David at the graduation ceremony in the back row of all the graduates, looking bored with the whole event and eager to get it over.

During the months when David lived with us, I got the opportunity to meet Melissa's adoptive mother, Josephine. She was now divorced from Melissa's adoptive father, Paul Carrington, and remarried to a man named Joe Brewer. I never had the opportunity to meet the Admiral. Josephine was living a short drive northeast of Kansas City, so we took David with us to see his grandmother in late 1978. In addition to this being my first meeting with Melissa's mother, it became a special meeting for Melissa, as well, as we were also going to meet her sister Barbara. It was quite a surprise for me to learn that Melissa's biological older sister had a relationship with Melissa's adoptive mother.

Apparently, Josephine had long-standing contact with Melissa's natural family and was now getting closer to Barbara and her family. The timing and details of how all this took place are sketchy to me, for I was never in the loop regarding anything on Melissa's side of the family. We had a good meeting with Joe and Josephine (or Jo as she was known) and Barbara, her husband, Brent, and their twin daughters Reina and Renee. Because Melissa was adopted by Josephine, I wasn't expecting the two of them to look alike. And they didn't. Josephine was a woman of small build and a slightly darker complexion, having been born in Mexico. Barbara looked more like Josephine than Melissa did, even though Barbara and Josephine were not related. Although Barbara and Melissa were sisters, they didn't bear any resemblance to each other in any way.

Over the years we continued to visit whenever we could, and we developed a much better relationship than one would expect, given the way the family had shut me out at the beginning of our marriage. Surprisingly, during these visits, no one ever shared any details about Melissa growing up with her adoptive family, or anything about her natural family that Barbara would have known about. Many times in our marriage, I asked Melissa why she didn't ask Barbara all kinds of questions about their parents and other relatives whom she had never met. Although they talked on the phone on a regular basis, Melissa told me she never wanted to talk about her birth family with Barbara.

In later years and from time to time, David, Dennis, and Suzan would be in need of some help for one thing or another, usually in the form of some money. I was more than willing to go along with whatever Melissa felt was appropriate to help her niece or nephews. Over time, however, I found myself asking why she felt so obligated to bail them out on so many occasions. I know she raised them as a mother, but it got on my nerves sometimes when they would send her Mother's Day cards or birthday cards addressed to "Mother." I respected her family relationships and put up with these annoyances, and even occasional Father's Day cards, from kids who were only a few years our junior.

TALK OF CHILDREN

Concerning the thought of becoming a father someday, Melissa and I were not particularly diligent to prevent pregnancy early in our marriage, but we weren't disappointed that we had no children. Although we both enjoyed spending time around kids, we really wondered whether we would make good parents. We always thought we would have our children in straight-jackets and would not do too well raising them, but I suppose most couples feel that way until they've had their first child and grow into that role. Eventually, we assumed that one of us must have had some medical reason why Melissa wasn't getting pregnant, but we didn't feel the need to investigate any further. Our thought was that this was our situation, and we accepted it as it was.

Melissa told me her doctor suggested that one of her car accidents may have caused some infertility problems. In later years, she asked me again if I was sorry that we didn't have children. Although I admitted it would have been fulfilling having a legacy carrying on after us, I said I was not disappointed and had no regrets. At times, I wondered if I was rationalizing our failure to have children. I wrestled with many thoughts in those early years of our marriage. *Would I have felt differently if I had married the "picture"? Did I feel that I didn't want to have children with Melissa, even though I was committed to our marriage for life? Did I believe it was unsafe for Melissa to have children without first losing some weight?*

Surprisingly, many years later in our marriage, Melissa again reported some news from her doctor as a result of her latest physical exam. There were indications that she had experienced more than one miscarriage. This news didn't hit me with any significant emotion that I could identify, but it implied we were about to be parents on more than one occasion. It wasn't the same as if a couple was expecting a baby for weeks or months before experiencing a devastating miscarriage. This discovery of ours was a fact out of the blue that I had a hard time taking to heart or getting emotional about.

MAKING ADJUSTMENTS

Despite sharing our love and friendship during the early years of our marriage, Melissa and I were still adjusting to each other and the differences that were such a surprise to me when we first met. Given my enjoyment for ice skating and tennis, I was disappointed that my own wife could not join me in either of these activities. I still was having some trouble expressing my love in a way that was consistent with all the words I had shared with Melissa before we ever met.

We agreed to a counseling telephone call with a married couple from our church. I selfishly expressed my desire to do more things with my wife than sit at home or visit with friends. This couple suggested other alternatives such as bowling, which would give us something more active to do, and would be more in line with what Melissa was physically capable of doing. After we had bowled a few times as a couple, Melissa joined a community bowling league where she received the "most improved team member" award.

Eventually, I adjusted my expectations and occasionally participated in skating or other activities by myself for exercise, but not as often as I wanted to. I was learning first-hand about the God kind of love, true love based on a decision to love someone that goes well

> We love because he first loved us.
> (1 John 4:19)

beyond those initial feelings of infatuation or loving someone for what they can do for you. God loves us first, and he helps us give that love to others.

I have to confess that these and other adjustments of expectations put a strain on us at different times through the years. In our first few months of marriage, I got very mad at something Melissa did or said and I had to leave the house for a while to cool off. I guess it was too easy for me to lay blame for any relationship issues on her deception before we ever got married. I had to continually remind myself that Melissa's deception, to delay my discovery of her sudden weight gain, was so she could "buy some time" and return to her normal weight before we ever met.

An even more serious example of how I'd express my anger was about twenty years into our marriage when I was riding my exercise bike in the basement of our house. I found myself crying out to God, *Lord, please take her or take me—something has to change.* Although I don't remember the reason why I expressed such a terrible thought, I suspect it was somehow wrapped up in this recurring flashback of how I first met Melissa. I asked God to forgive me of this momentary and shameful thought, and I never shared this private moment with anyone during the rest of our marriage.

Although I had forgiven Melissa for misleading me during our initial six-month phone relationship in 1976, I occasionally found myself reliving in my mind all that had happened. Each time I relived it, I had to forgive Melissa all over again, and then ask God's forgiveness for not having put this behind me. The Bible does teach about forgiving someone many times, but I was forgiving Melissa of the same offense over and over and failing to forget what she had done, as God forgets what we have done.

I stored away the pictures I had of Melissa when she was thinner; however, those pictures occasionally became a topic

> For I will forgive their wickedness and will remember their sins no more.
> (Jeremiah 31:34)

of conversation. One day, I had the larger, framed picture of Melissa out of storage for some reason. When she saw the photograph she insisted I destroy it. As I agreed to her request, I must have been yearning for that woman of the picture. It wasn't easy to tear it up. Reluctantly, I carried out her wishes and destroyed that symbol of someone who didn't exist anymore. Without saying anything to Melissa, I stored away her wallet-sized photographs in a small box, where they remained throughout the remainder of our marriage.

As I became more accepting of our circumstances, and came to view Melissa as only "Melissa," we would sometimes come in contact with people who viewed us differently. With my appearing to be younger, we occasionally had to endure some embarrassing situations when out in public. On one of our many trips to garage sales, I was trying to decide whether I wanted to buy something, while Melissa was already making her purchases. The homeowner at the garage sale asked Melissa, "Is your son going to buy something also?"

"He's my husband," Melissa replied rather harshly.

We quickly exited that uncomfortable situation. It became an important habit throughout our marriage to introduce ourselves quickly as husband and wife whenever the relationship might be misinterpreted.

CHAPTER 7

Maturing as Husband and Wife

My next Air Force assignment was at Ellsworth Air Force Base, South Dakota. After four and a half years at my first assignment, it was time to move on. As was our pattern at Dickie Goober, at the new location, we first had to get an apartment off base while we waited our turn to get assigned on-base housing. Once again, I grabbed the hammer and nails and followed Melissa's direction on where to hang everything as she decorated our new home.

Melissa enjoyed home parties for anything from Tupperware and Home Interiors, to Mary Kay makeup products. This tied in very well with her decorating ability and her love for working on all sorts of crafts. After moving to South Dakota, she began receiving unemployment pay from Kansas. Knowing that this money was not going to last forever, Melissa started her quest to come up with new ideas for earning money through her artistic skills in crafts.

Over the years, she made crafts in assembly-line fashion and attended local craft shows to sell her wares. Starting in Belton, she had also become skilled in quilting, tole painting, cross-stitching, and crocheting. Usually those treasured creations were not for sale at any price because they became gifts for close family and friends. I was proud of Melissa's ability to create so many beautiful things for decorations in each apartment or house over the years. I always looked forward to returning home after work or after returning from some out of town trip. Our home represented a beautiful sanctuary from the world around us.

Another moneymaking opportunity Melissa got deeply involved in for several years was refunding. She saved all her product labels so she would be ready to send off for a refund as soon as one became available. Once she got addicted to this hobby, any trip to the store required us to search for new refund offers. While we lived at Ellsworth, Melissa hit a gold mine when a fellow refunder sold Melissa all her refund labels, or refund trash, as I used to call it. Instead of a few shoeboxes and bags full of labels, Melissa now had to set aside an entire room for her refunding hobby. She was accomplished at remembering all these refund offers, keeping track of which labels were needed, whether she had enough of those labels, and so on. I used to tell her that if she applied these same skills to studying the Bible, she would know the Word inside and out.

Our move to Ellsworth, just outside of Rapid City, South Dakota, provided opportunities to see the Black Hills and Mount Rushmore, among several other tourist attractions. We also experienced extremely serious winter conditions and high winds. It was quite a sight to see a line of several B-52 bombers fighting the cross-winds making takeoffs and landings, in preparation for a military scenario we hoped would never come to pass. Our church home during the majority of this assignment was at the Lord's Chapel, a nondenominational congregation in downtown Rapid City. We met many good friends at church and at the base, and we were getting very well settled into our relationship together as veterans of more than four years of marriage.

The assignment at Ellsworth was short-lived. We spent only twenty months there before I was selected for an unaccompanied short-tour assignment to South Korea. The thought of spending a year apart at this stage in our marriage was disconcerting, but it was something that many military members before and after us had to deal with. Until this tour in Korea, our longest time apart had been three or four weeks for various training courses at Keesler. We were confident, though, that we would manage to get through this assignment separation. Melissa and I decided she would move to St. Louis, up the street from my parents, while I was stationed on the other side of the world in Korea.

Short Tour to Korea

I was assigned to Osan Air Base, where I had many exciting opportunities for taking pictures in the local villages around the base and in the large city of Seoul. I got deeply involved in a local Christian Servicemen's Center ministry, which provided some home-cooked meals, fellowship, and activities with other Air Force members stationed at Osan, some with and some without their families. On Sundays, we all supported the on-base chapel programs and services.

While I was keeping busy with my Air Force work in Korea and maintaining Christian fellowship and accountability, Melissa was not achieving the same result on the home front. She spent most of her days working on her refunding hobby, and from time to time she visited the nearby family members. Unfortunately, she wasn't making the effort to get out to church on a regular basis, if at all. Before I left for Korea, we had some time to get connected with a church and a home group that I prayed would keep her involved while I was gone. But the fact that she didn't drive gave her an excuse to stay home from church—although she managed to get around town for things when she really wanted to. Melissa kept to herself concerning any spiritual growth during this time.

The one and only time she drove during our marriage was once while I was in Korea. A couple friends of hers that she met through refunding decided to take her out one evening. One of her friends drove our car, which was otherwise sitting in the parking lot while I was away. They went to, of all places, a drinking establishment with male dancers in Illinois. To hear Melissa tell the story, I believe she wanted out of there fast, but she couldn't leave on her own. When the time came to go home, her friends were in no shape to drive back to Missouri, so Melissa was elected as the unlicensed designated driver.

With hands shaking, she slowly navigated the car toward home. Along the journey, she encountered a highway patrolman who pulled her over. Melissa tightly gripped the steering wheel as she tried to stop shaking. She had no driver's license, and she had two drunks in the back seat. The patrolman approached the car.

"Ma'am, are you okay?"

"Yes, I'm just trying to get my two friends home safely."

"Well, you were driving too slow back there. You need to pick up the pace a little bit," the officer admonished.

The officer never once asked for her driver's license, and he let her drive away. Melissa safely reached the parking space at our apartment. She got out of the car and left her friends there to sleep it off until they were sober enough to find their own cars and drive home.

An unexpected blessing of my assignment to Korea was that I was able to finish up the required college credits that made me eligible to apply for the Airman Education and Commissioning Program. I had continued my one- or two-at-a-time coursework at Ellsworth and now, with some highly compressed course schedules, I was able to complete several courses during my time in Korea. While I was on leave back home in St. Louis, Melissa and I discussed our options, prayed, and concluded that I should apply for the commissioning program.

When I returned to Korea, I completed the application process, including another full medical exam, and I was selected for the program. Having by then been promoted to Technical Sergeant, I would remain at that grade level while attending the University of Missouri at Rolla (now called the Missouri University of Science and Technology) for three years. In order for me to start the fall semester on time, I was able to shorten my tour in Korea by two months.

PROFESSIONAL COLLEGE STUDENT

Melissa coordinated the entire move to Rolla by herself. She found a house to rent in the town, coordinated with the Air Force to schedule the move, and had all our household goods packed up and delivered to the rental house before I ever got home—all this from a woman who didn't even drive. This was our only household move where I didn't have to lift a finger until it was time to unpack. It was a blessing that Melissa was able to do all this before I returned from Korea. In this and many other situations, she was representative of the "Proverbs 31 woman" mentioned in Proverbs—a woman of high character who fears the Lord and is industrious in maintaining a home of refuge for her family.

I was back in Missouri again for my next Air Force assignment as a full-time college student in Rolla. Living near St. Louis meant we were able to be with my sister Pat when she was first diagnosed with cancer. At the time, she and her husband were planning to start a family. Then they learned she couldn't have children due to this terrible disease. Pat began a decade-long

A wife of noble character who can find? She is worth far more than rubies. Her husband has full confidence in her and lacks nothing of value. She brings him good, not harm, all the days of her life. She selects wool and flax and works with eager hands. She is like the merchant ships, bringing her food from afar. She gets up while it is still dark; she provides food for her family . . . She opens her arms to the poor and extends her hands to the needy . . . Charm is deceptive, and beauty is fleeting; but a woman who fears the LORD is to be praised. (Proverbs 31:10–15, 20, 30)

battle for her life, which would involve numerous surgeries and cancer treatments over the years.

Starting full-time college as a married, twenty-six-year-old student had some advantages. For one, I didn't have to deal with all the distractions younger students faced. I also had Melissa's encouragement and support through everything. Although it was extremely hard work, and long hours of study in a jam-packed academic schedule, Melissa was the reason I was able to do as well as I did. She fully understood that I had to dedicate myself to doing the best I could and supported me every step of the way. My fellow Air Force classmates and I had a few informal and formal events to attend, and periodic meetings. But our primary focus was to study and complete our programs on schedule while keeping our grades above the minimum levels set by the Air Force.

Melissa and I became members of the Word of Faith Tabernacle, a nondenominational church that expanded into a new building shortly after we arrived. As a full-time student,

I had some limitations on my time, but we were able to grow in our knowledge of God's Word through a consistent church home for all three years. Several of the church members were connected in some way with the university, so I would frequently run into them around campus during the week. Melissa and I opened up our home to host a church fellowship group, and this enabled us to be a blessing to the church as we shared in the blessings the Lord had provided us in our marriage.

During this school assignment, Melissa and I obtained our military medical and commissary support from Ft. Leonard Wood Army Post, about twenty-five miles southwest of Rolla. During a visit to the doctor, Melissa was diagnosed with diabetes. It started out fairly benign and initially she took pills to control her blood sugar. Gradually, however, over the succeeding years, the treatment progressed to insulin shots, and she began to experience other health complications.

When May 1985 arrived, I graduated summa cum laude with a bachelor of science degree in computer science. This was all thanks to God's blessings and Melissa's strong support and encouragement. Within a few weeks, I was headed back to San Antonio, Texas, for Officer Training School. Once again, Melissa and I missed each other very much while we had to be apart for more training. Twelve weeks later, Melissa, Mom, and Dad joined me at Lackland Air Force Base as we celebrated the completion of another milestone in my Air Force career and our married lives.

BACK TO THE HOME FRONT

My first assignment as an officer was across the Mississippi River from St. Louis, at Scott Air Force Base. I began the second half of my Air Force career as a computer officer in an organization providing programming support for the Military Airlift

Command's airlift planning software. I was involved in many new activities as a junior officer, in addition to my computer role as a hands-on programmer and team leader for various software projects. In line with my previous drive to get my undergraduate degree and be commissioned as an officer, my career goal now was to obtain a master's degree. I also thought about a future teaching assignment at the Air Force Academy.

The Air Force Institute of Technology offered an in-residence master's degree program at Wright-Patterson Air Force Base in Ohio. I began the process of identifying myself as a volunteer for such an assignment. With God having blessed my success at the undergraduate level, and having enabled me to be a distinguished graduate of Officer Training School, I believed my eventual selection seemed promising. In the meantime, I pursued an interview at the Academy with the possibility that I might be selected to get my master's degree at a civilian institution, with a follow-on assignment to teach at the Air Force Academy. I was invited to come out to the Academy at my own expense for an interview, and that alone was worth the price of admission. It was quite impressive to walk the hallways of this institution that I had dreamed about for so many years.

Unfortunately, I was not selected for an immediate graduate degree program sponsored by the Academy. When I followed up with the assignments officer a few weeks later, it appeared that my eleven years' prior service time might prevent me from being selected for the in-residence program as well. As usual, Melissa was there by my side to encourage me and help me work through these changing expectations. She was ready to help me keep pressing toward my goal or to adjust to another path. I charted a new path and started a night school graduate degree program. As an officer, I knew I would ultimately need a master's degree on my resume to make more advanced promotions possible.

It took us a few months to settle into a local church in the area around Scott Air Force Base, but God eventually led us to the Belleville Assembly of God, where we got deeply involved in Sunday school programs, church activities, and hosting a fellowship group in our home. It was at this time that Melissa finally quit smoking. She had stopped for a while when we lived in Rapid City, but some well-meaning friend left a cigarette or two with her and she started smoking again.

During a sermon at Belleville Assembly, the pastor used an analogy describing Mary holding a cigarette in her hand with Jesus on her lap. Perhaps due to Melissa's Catholic upbringing, this disturbing visual image hit home with her and she immediately stopped smoking. In addition to the positive influence of our church, we also participated in an Officers' Christian Fellowship group at the base. This continued our connection with the ministry we first discovered during my undergraduate days in Rolla.

Despite Melissa's own challenges in dealing with the news of her adoption before we got married, and other family issues she would never talk about, she was always there for me when I had some difficult times in my own family. In early 1987, such a difficult event occurred. My mother once again attempted suicide, this time by taking a handful of pills. Fortunately, my father found her in time and got her to the hospital immediately. She ended up in a coma for many days and stayed in the hospital for more than a month to recover fully. Melissa was by my side throughout the whole ordeal with her loving support to my family and me.

BILOXI—TOGETHER THIS TIME

My career field was in transition at the time I graduated from Officer Training School in 1985. Our training class was allowed to go to our initial assignments directly, instead of first attending a four-month-long Communications Computer Officer Course, at Keesler Air Force Base. Eventually, the Air

Force would require each of us to attend that course at Keesler. By June 1987, I was back at my old stomping grounds, as an officer this time, attending one more technical school. Because this training was not as demanding on our daily schedule as some other training courses, Melissa and I rented an apartment outside the base in Biloxi. This meant we had to pay double rent during this time, but it was well worth it. We were together in Mississippi during this long training course, and we were able to do some sightseeing in the area on weekends.

Among other weekend trips that included going to Pensacola, Florida, and Mobile, Alabama, Melissa and I drove to New Orleans. And, of course, we went to Chalmette, Louisiana, where Melissa spent many years growing up. I took pictures of the French Quarter during the daytime and many other historic sites around New Orleans. We drove down to Chalmette, where I took some pictures of the historic Chalmette National Cemetery, adjacent to the site of the Civil War Battle of New Orleans. We learned about the history of the area, but we saw nothing that had any personal connection to Melissa's childhood.

I looked at people dressed in period costumes and others around Chalmette, and I wondered if any of them knew Melissa's family when she was growing up down there. It was very unusual that she did not want to stop anywhere in town and would not even point out anything specific as we drove through the town. I later thought as we were headed back to Biloxi, *What had happened in Chalmette years before that made Melissa want to keep on driving just now, and not even show me any of her memories of that town?*

Once again, I was puzzled and confused. I asked my wife a few questions, but I heard no satisfactory answers. It became clear that this was another one of those "don't ask" situations.

CHAPTER 8

Achieving Lifelong Goals

In the summer of 1988, I obtained an early selection for in-residence Squadron Officer's School, at Maxwell Air Force Base, Alabama. This was a nine-week course during which Melissa, once again, had to hold down the fort by herself, providing yet another example of how supportive she was to me through all the challenges of military life. My non-driving wife had to manage the household in my absence, and she continued demonstrating her keen ability to find transportation around town when she needed it, through family and friends.

Shortly before I completed this training course, I received the unexpected, but very welcomed, news that I had been selected to attend the Air Force Institute of Technology graduate program in Ohio. The news was unexpected because I previously thought this program was out of my reach. My report date wasn't until the following May, so we had plenty of time to plan the next move.

When May 1989 came along, we were headed east to Dayton, Ohio, and Wright-Patterson Air Force Base. I took an intense course of study during the next eighteen months, and once again, God blessed me with Melissa's unwavering support.

During this assignment, I pinned on the rank of captain and finally achieved a nickname I had inherited in high school when some fellow hockey players learned I was going into the Air Force: Captain Jim Bob.

Despite the very demanding graduate school program, Melissa and I managed to fit in some sightseeing around the area. The most important attraction in Ohio for Melissa was the Longaberger basket factory near Columbus. It was during my assignment in Dayton when she began selling handmade Longaberger baskets. She was able to take a bus tour up to Dresden, Ohio, where the factory was located. What started out as a few baskets purchased at a home party turned into a houseful of baskets many years later.

We began our church experience in Dayton with a local nondenominational congregation, where we had good Christian fellowship and teaching. We made several friends who were also in the Air Force and doing graduate work. Although this was only an eighteen-month assignment at the institute, the Lord led us to another church for the latter portion of our time in Ohio. At the Dayton Assembly of God Church, Melissa became involved in Sunday school administration—sometimes overly involved. She frequently got so engrossed while working on the record keeping that I had to pull her away to go into the Sunday morning church service. Despite my busy school schedule, I was able to teach a young boys' Sunday school class, and both Melissa and I supported a number of other church activities.

Nebraska, Not Colorado

As a distinguished graduate of the Air Force Institute of Technology, with a newly minted master of science degree in computer science, I had hoped my next assignment might be directly to the Air Force Academy. Instead, it turned out we were headed farther north to Offutt Air Force Base in Omaha, Nebraska, the home of the Strategic Air Command. We arrived in December of 1990. When I started in my new position at the beginning of the year, I was providing computer software support for the nuclear war planning mission of the Strategic Air Command, and later the United States Strategic Command, as it would become known.

Always looking ahead to the next Air Force career goal, I still had a desire to seek out a teaching position at the Academy. With that in mind, I also pursued a selection for a PhD degree slot back at the Air Force Institute of Technology in Ohio, where I had been previously assigned. This pursuit led to a funded interview trip back to Wright-Patterson Air Force Base the following year. Although the faculty at the Institute of Technology were well aware of my eleven years of prior enlisted time, the key concern coming out of that interview, and the reason for my not being selected, was the risk I posed by being retirement-eligible much sooner than the other candidates. Therefore, I put that idea behind me and continued keeping my application current for an Academy teaching position as I carried out my job responsibilities in Nebraska.

Melissa continued her activity in local crafts shows and involvement in Longaberger baskets. Although she didn't try selling many baskets, she kept enough business going to allow her to get her own baskets at a reduced rate. They were reproducing around our house like rabbits and appearing on every shelf or cabinet where there was room to place them.

My assignment in Omaha put us much closer to Melissa's mother living near Kansas City, so we were able to visit several times. Each time we visited Josephine and Melissa's stepfather, Joe, we came home with some more bits and pieces of Josephine's Mexican heritage. Pictures of Mexican generals and old family photos and collectibles provided a glimpse into

Melissa's adoptive mother's side of the family. Sometimes, it appeared that Melissa had other items from her mother that she didn't want me to see. I didn't snoop around to find out what they were.

Whether these hidden items were pictures or not, I wasn't sure. A few times, I came across some pictures of people I didn't recognize, or pictures of people who looked like someone related to Melissa. Once again, this became an area to stay clear of, as she got very upset if I asked too many questions. Melissa would get nervous whenever I would have to fill out any Air Force paperwork requiring family history. If I received an award or promotion and the Air Force offered to do a hometown news release, she never wanted that news released in any hometown other than St. Louis. After I allowed Melissa to maintain these boundaries for so many years, it became harder to make an issue out of anything that still didn't make sense. On the other hand, the more I allowed these mysteries to pile up, the more I felt I should start digging deeper, even though it seemed a little too late.

Melissa and I found a great church home in Omaha at the Southside Assembly of God. We established many friendships and got involved in several of the church ministries. Melissa once again found a role she enjoyed, working in Sunday school administration. While at Southside Assembly, I accepted an invitation to go down to the Academy for another instructor interview. Soon after that interview trip, I discovered that a fellow Southside member was also seeking an assignment to the computer science department. His name was James, and he was a younger lieutenant, so I could identify with his perspective, based on my first Academy interview years before. A key difference was that James already had his graduate degree, so either one of us could be selected for a direct assignment. As the selection process continued, we ultimately learned it was down to a choice between the two of us. This situation was the source of some humor, as we tried to relieve the underlying tension.

"Hey, James, I have a prayer request for you," I jokingly said to him.

"Sure, Jim, what would you like me to pray for?" James asked with a smile on his face, as he knew where I was headed.

"Well, I'd like you to pray that God would bless me with this teaching assignment to the Air Force Academy."

"Well, sure, Jim, I'll be sure to put that on my prayer list. Could you pray with me about something also?"

"Of course."

"Pray that the other guy in the running for this assignment to the Academy won't be devastated when I get selected," James said with a large grin on his face.

"Okay, James. You can be sure that I'll be praying for that other guy every day."

Although we had some fun kidding each other about this whole situation, we trusted God for his will to be done for both of us concerning this assignment selection.

SELECTED FOR ACADEMY ASSIGNMENT

In early 1993, I received a call from the computer science department personnel officer informing me that I had been selected for the Academy teaching position. Given my long history of trying to get to the Academy, I was absolutely thrilled with the news. So although I didn't get there as a cadet, I would reach the Academy as an instructor. Shortly after getting this wonderful news from the Academy, I got a surprising call from the Air Force Institute of Technology.

"Captain Marr, would you consider taking a short-notice PhD school slot? The original candidate had to turn down the assignment, and your name came up as a potential replacement."

I could hardly believe my ears. What a tough decision I had before me.

"I'll have to discuss this first with my wife. I'll give you a call tomorrow to let you know what we decide."

Melissa and I discussed this opportunity at length that night and prayed together for God to guide us in the proper decision. Because I had already given my answer to the Academy and because that had been my original desire, we agreed that I should turn down the offer for a PhD program. I'm sure Melissa didn't mind the fact that she wouldn't have to be a school widow for three more years.

Before leaving my assignment at Strategic Command, I was providing some training for a newly arrived captain in our work area. Somewhere in the conversation, she mentioned that she had turned down a PhD slot at the last minute. Coincidentally, that was the very same school slot offered to me a few weeks before her arrival.

In May 1993, I was reassigned to the Air Force Academy. It was an awe-inspiring experience when I first walked around the Academy training area. I couldn't help but feel like pinching myself to make sure it was real. The daily demands of teaching multiple sections of computer classes, grading papers, and performing additional duties would occasionally take the edge off some of those lofty feelings. To sharpen my inspiration, I would simply take a walk on the terrazzo, or watch a noontime formation of cadets. These brief moments reminded me of the significance of what I was doing there at the Academy, not to mention recognizing God's hand in the long journey it took to get to that point in my life.

Right next to me, through it all, was Melissa, providing loving encouragement at each step. She always supported my constant drive to reach one goal after another. She also was there to comfort me a couple of years later when my sister Pat was in the final stages of a twelve-year battle with cancer.

Knowing that Melissa and I could only be back in St. Louis for a few days, I wrestled with a tough decision. Should I go home immediately to be with Pat while she was still alive, or should I be ready to travel home for her memorial service? I had the opportunity to talk to my sister on the phone a few days before, and we had discussed our trust in God for his promise of healing. But we both knew that departing to be with the Lord in heaven was the ultimate healing.

On February 11, 1995, Dad called to give me the news that Pat was at home with the Lord. Melissa and I flew to St. Louis to be with the family and attend Pat's memorial service on Valentine's Day. Although I struggled to hold it together, during the service I managed to read a letter I had written to Pat. I knew she was at peace with God, but we missed her so much. Melissa was there by my side to help me through those emotions, the same emotions I would in coming years have to deal with in our own relationship as husband and wife.

Living in Colorado Springs put us near Rawlins, Wyoming, and Dennis, Suzan, and David. Eventually, Suzan left Rawlins and we didn't have much contact with her for about ten years. Melissa and I drove up to Rawlins several times and we visited with Dennis and David and their growing families when they came down to see us in Colorado.

Transition to Civilian Life

As I was nearing the end of my Academy assignment, many officers were offered early retirements at fifteen years of service. I decided that retiring at the twenty-two-year point was the best decision. Although I had been selected for promotion to the rank of Major, it would be at least a year before I could pin on the rank, and a couple more years on active duty to retain that rank at retirement. I also knew in the next year we would have to move away from Colorado Springs, something that Melissa and I were not prepared to do. This decision allowed me to retire when I was forty and get started sooner on a civilian career. In a few years' time, the decision to settle down in a stable location would become extremely important in dealing with Melissa's health challenges.

In 1996, I retired from the Air Force and initially got a job at MCI, which later became WorldCom. After six years at WorldCom as a systems analyst, the newsmaking events of Bernie Ebbers caught up with me in a 2002 downsize, and I was laid off. I had always been loyal to my employer. During the good times when some people jumped from one job to another, I always said, "I'll be here until they kick me out." Little did I know how prophetic those words would become.

Melissa took this layoff pretty hard. For the first time in our marriage, I was unemployed and she didn't like it for one minute. Not surprising, it was Melissa who eventually thought of someone I could contact about possible employment. Despite the layoff, the Lord was faithful, and I was hired into a new position as a systems engineer in Colorado Springs within two months, immediately making higher pay than I did at WorldCom. It was quite a blessing, and it was just like God to turn a layoff into an advancement opportunity.

When Melissa and I first arrived in Colorado Springs, the Lord led us to the Austin Bluffs Assembly of God Church. We got deeply involved in various ministries, serving on the church board, teaching Sunday school, organizing fellowship group dinners, ushering, participating in women's ministries, and hosting fellowship groups in our home. Naturally, it was with mixed feelings when we followed the Lord's leading out of that church and into Grace Fellowship Church, which later was renamed Church For All Nations.

At our new church, I got involved right away in the media ministry, doing camera work during the three weekly services. Melissa primarily attended the Sunday morning service only, until she later hosted a women's Bible study in our home so she could have some Christian fellowship without having to travel outside the house. As she began experiencing declining health, it became more uncomfortable for her to attend church, to the point that she eventually stopped attending completely.

CHAPTER 9

Declining Health

The first sign that Melissa's health was beginning to change for the worse was a gradual decrease in her ability to go up and down stairs. Although we started in a four-level home when we first moved to Colorado Springs, we eventually made the transition to a one-level floor plan to minimize the number of stairs Melissa would have to navigate.

EYESIGHT AFFECTED NEXT

In 2003, Melissa's eyesight began to deteriorate significantly. I had to make several business trips for my employer that year and I had to prefill her insulin syringes before each trip. This was because she couldn't see the syringe markings clearly enough to get the right dosage of insulin. Melissa also started having retina issues requiring hundreds of laser shots over several visits to stop retinal bleeding, which was interfering with her eyesight. For a short period of time, Melissa was trying out some special glasses designed to counter macular degeneration, and I allowed some negative thoughts to linger in my mind about what might happen if she lost her eyesight completely.

Thankfully, the retina treatments stabilized her eyesight and she was able to get around the house reasonably well.

Melissa's declining eyesight was only the beginning of many diabetes-related complications, but it soon became the cause of several arguments about the cleanliness of the house. I usually did most of the serious cleaning around the house throughout our marriage. Some of my innate perfectionist tendencies were made more intense by my spit-and-polish Air Force training. I had mellowed out over the years and tried to avoid getting stressed out about minor things. But as Melissa's eyesight declined, I realized I had to keep closer attention on things around the house. Usually, she argued that I was making it all up and that she had already cleaned the kitchen, bathroom, or some other area of the house. Unfortunately, I couldn't let things go, as this was getting to be a serious problem. In time, to avoid the confrontations and maintain some peace in the home, I had to resort to cleaning things behind her back.

These cleaning incidents provided more justification for Melissa to accuse me on occasion of being critical of her. She would say, "I'm doing the best I can." Throughout our marriage, my attempts to help her improve in various ways usually were interpreted as being hyper-critical. That was an area I struggled with repeatedly. I always wondered how much of this was rooted in the way we met and any lingering feelings I was harboring about Melissa not being the person I fell in love with. It was true she was doing the best she could, but I couldn't ignore that she needed some help. She hired various friends to help with the cleaning and other tasks around the house while I was at work or out of town. This helped Melissa feel better because she was taking some of the load off me.

While dealing with her declining eyesight, Melissa was having increased discomfort with hip and back pain, as well as weakness in her legs. While these were clear and identifiable pains, the doctor could never identify a specific cause of the pain. When shopping to get a new recliner for Melissa, we decided it was prudent to get a lift-chair. This kind of chair would make it easier for her to sit down and get up again, which would be especially important if she had any additional decline in her leg strength.

Eventually, that chair became invaluable, as it enabled Melissa to retain some independence around the house, when she could no longer get up from any other chair by herself.

Getting to Know the Paramedics

On a few occasions, Melissa lost her footing in the house and ended up on her knees, or flat on the floor. The first time, she was alone and was able to crawl to the bed and get back on her feet by herself. Another time, it happened when I was at home and I managed to help her get up off the floor. Eventually, such occurrences required assistance from the paramedics to ensure she hadn't hurt herself by falling, and to avoid injury from me or a neighbor trying to lift her incorrectly. The first time we called in the paramedics was a most difficult situation, but also a most humorous one. My brilliant idea to get Melissa on her feet only made it worse.

One night before going to bed, Melissa was in the bathroom. I heard some loud noises and ran to see what had happened. I discovered her sitting on the floor of the bathroom with the shower curtain draped over her shoulders. While trying to get up from the toilet, she'd lost her balance and grabbed for the curtain as she went down. At first, I tried to reposition Melissa where we could both work together to get her off the floor, but neither one of us was strong enough to lift her up. We thought about getting a neighbor to come over and help us, but I was concerned that we might hurt her arms if we tried to pull her up incorrectly.

A brilliant idea popped into my head. I thought we could get Melissa to slide over to the basement steps that were around the corner from the bathroom. She could hang her legs down the stairway, plant her feet on a step, and simply stand up. Under normal conditions, this might have worked, but by the time we tried this, Melissa was just too weak. I had to get her something to snack on to avoid a low blood sugar episode. As I tried repeatedly to help her stand up to her feet on the stairs, she couldn't do it, and she ended up sliding down a step or two at each attempt. This continued over the next half hour or so until we ended up all the way to the basement floor. Obviously, it was time to call 911. Because this was the first time I had ever called 911, it was humbling to admit the need for this help, but there was no question that we needed it.

When the paramedics arrived, I quickly directed them down to the basement, where Melissa sat on the floor leaning on some pillows. As they were assessing Melissa's medical condition, I was careful to let her answer all their questions herself. The appearance of her sitting on the basement floor like this may have raised some concerns in their minds, and so I felt this was not the time to speak for Melissa. Fortunately, they could see that she had not fallen. Because she was coherent—albeit very weak—the paramedics didn't raise any issues after she explained how she got on the floor.

So back to the original problem. How were the paramedics going to get Melissa on her feet and back up the stairs?

They brought in a special stirrup that they positioned under Melissa. The strongest three in the group carefully lifted her into this stirrup and slowly struggled step-by-step to move her back up the stairs and into her bed. After confirming that she was not injured and didn't require any medical treatment, the paramedics departed, thus ending our first of several such experiences over the following years.

Melissa initially borrowed a walker from a friend to use around the house, but eventually I got her a walker of her own, as she increasingly needed more stability to avoid falling down. When going to doctor appointments, we started borrowing wheelchairs at their offices. Later, to ensure I would always have a chair available to push Melissa to and from her appointments, I bought an ambulatory chair. When the few steps from our house to our garage became impossible to navigate, we had an elevator chairlift installed that allowed her to ride up and down the stairs while still sitting in a chair.

As Melissa was having increasing health challenges, we avoided talking about her long-term prognosis. This was a topic she never wanted to discuss. As her mobility became more limited, we shared many hours together watching our favorite television shows each evening. This was something we could enjoy together as husband and wife and as best friends. I regret that we didn't spend more time confessing healing Scriptures out loud each night and spending more time in prayer together, but we stayed close to each other through these extremely trying times.

TIME FOR CATARACT SURGERY

By early 2005, Melissa had a final visit to her retina doctor. She emerged from that appointment, navigating her walker through the doorway, and began sharing the good news.

"The doctor said I don't need any more retina treatments. We finally got all of it under control."

After acknowledging this great news, I could see Melissa was upset about something.

"But now I need to have cataract surgery on both eyes."

As I was trying to process the severity of this announcement, we continued to walk slowly through the waiting room toward the exit. People were reading magazines, talking to family members, or looking up with a polite smile as we made our way past them. With so many people around us, I wanted Melissa to wait until we got out to our van, where we could discuss everything in private.

Melissa was too upset to wait. "What are we going to do? Talk to me!"

Under my breath, I said, "Please, Melissa, let's get down to the van before we talk about all this." It was always difficult for me to have a private conversation in public, and this upset her very much. "Melissa, we'll have to take it a step at a time and trust God to help us get through it."

As God was faithful to help with each challenge we faced, he gave us the strength to work through the situation one step at a time and one eye at a time. We started with the pre-op doctor visits, the surgery visit, and the follow-up visits for the first eye. As Melissa was about to begin the same sequence for the other eye, she had to postpone the surgery appointment when she experienced unusual symptoms of weakness and lack of energy. She decided to go see her primary care doctor in May 2005, and was diagnosed with congestive heart failure—too much water retention was putting a strain on her heart. This was the first sign of her kidneys beginning to fail from the long-term diabetes. Her doctor got her admitted to the cardiac care center at the hospital that same night.

We had borrowed a wheelchair to get Melissa back out to the parking lot. We were both nearly crying from frustration as we struggled to get her feet up into our van. The water retention had been building up in her legs to the point where she could barely bend them enough to get into the seat.

A kind man came by to help us. "I understand exactly what you are going through. My wife had similar health conditions for many years."

Little did we know that night how much experience the two of us would gain over the next two years with doctors and hospitals and medical treatments.

After stopping by the house to quickly pack a bag of things for Melissa, we arrived at the hospital about 7:00 P.M. That night of getting Melissa through a battery of tests at the cardiac center, and eventually up to a patient room, became the longest night without sleep we had ever experienced together. When we got to her room around 4:00 A.M., I had been awake for twenty-four hours straight. The stress and sleep deprivation caught up with me and I broke down.

At home I had been helping Melissa get in and out of bed, and I didn't see how she was going to do this at the hospital. I didn't expect her to get enough attention from the nurses because they were always so busy. I felt helpless. I knew I had to go home and get some sleep, but I didn't want to leave Melissa alone in that hospital. I was the only one who knew what she needed, and we had developed our routines in the midst of such trying circumstances. Melissa convinced me that she would manage with the nurses' help, so I left the hospital and drove home. It was an incredibly emotional trip driving back home as I was crying out to God for help. I couldn't see how we would deal with all

Cast all your anxiety on him because he cares for you. (1 Peter 5:7)

No temptation has seized you except what is common to man. And God is faithful; he will not let you be tempted beyond what you can bear. But when you are tempted, he will also provide a way out so that you can stand up under it. (1 Corinthians 10:13)

this, but God would help us bear the load and he would ensure we weren't crushed by the temptation to give up.

GOD HELPING US TO ADAPT

While our situation didn't improve, God was changing our attitude and helping us manage day by day. Although the challenges to our faith gradually worsened, we were able to adapt to our new lifestyle. Melissa remained in the hospital for five days, and she endured several heart tests and other evaluations to determine what treatment was needed for her condition. During one of the consultations at her hospital bed, her cardiologist advised her on overall health issues. He commented, "Melissa, the extra weight you carry now is putting a heavy demand on your heart. I'm sure your husband would love to see you back at the weight you were when you first got married."

The doctor wrongly assumed that when Melissa and I were first married thirty years ago, she had been much thinner, and she had let her weight continually increase. The truth, however, was that other than the more recent water retention from kidney failure, Melissa actually weighed less than when we were first married.

We frowned and glanced at each other, but neither one of us said anything.

After the doctor left the room, she whispered, "I don't like that doctor anymore."

When Melissa went home from the hospital, she left with several follow-up appointments for the heart doctor, the kidney doctor, and the sleep center to verify her new prescription to use oxygen at night. Shortly after this hospital stay, I created the first version of a lengthy medications list on the computer, because it was becoming so hard to keep her doctors informed about all the different prescription medicine she was taking.

The list usually contained at least fifteen different medications addressing a variety of conditions, from anemia, low potassium, vitamin levels, and high blood pressure, to an underactive thyroid, water retention, uneven blood sugar levels, dry eyes, itching, and pain relief. One of my weekly tasks was to fill up Melissa's large pillbox with all the medications she needed to take each day, as well as preparing insulin and anti-anemia injections.

Fortunately, the sleep study confirmed Melissa didn't have sleep apnea or any other conditions requiring special devices beyond using the oxygen machine at night. By August of 2005, she was caught up on all her other appointments and was strong enough to get her second cataract surgery completed. With that second eye surgery behind her, we had to wait for the eye to heal sufficiently before she could get her eyeglass prescription updated. During this waiting period, Melissa got by with either using or not using her glasses depending on what she was doing. To make it easier for her to use the computer with her declining vision, I purchased some special magnification and talking software, which made it possible for her to send a few e-mails, or maybe search for a recipe on a Web site.

Gradually, Melissa stopped using the computer entirely. This was not only for vision reasons, but also because it was becoming unsafe and exhausting for her to get up from the desk chair by herself. This decline in function and mobility happened so slowly that I didn't even notice the first time she encountered a new limitation. Only in retrospect did we see how our lives had changed dramatically through these medical challenges. In the coming year, Melissa's existence became limited almost exclusively to the bed, the lift-chair, and the bathroom.

She was able to get out to doctor appointments, so this meant she wasn't totally homebound. With all the diuretic pills

Melissa was taking, however, she always had to be aware of where the next bathroom stop would be. For the doctor visits, we had the timing and locations down cold. We knew exactly where to find each of the one-person bathrooms, where I could assist. By this time, she was unable to go into a women's bathroom on her own. Although we were both well aware of this limitation, Melissa got upset that we no longer went anywhere other than the doctor's office.

"Why don't we ever go out to a restaurant anymore, or take a drive somewhere?" Melissa asked.

"What will we do when you have to go to the bathroom, Melissa? I can't help you get into a bathroom in a restaurant or at a rest stop."

"Are you embarrassed to be seen with me using my walker or in my wheelchair?"

"Of course not. It's just too impractical to do those things right now."

I think this realization of how limited her life had become suddenly hit Melissa at this moment. At no other time before that realization had she even asked to go anywhere. It went without saying that going out in public wasn't very practical. Melissa never brought this up again.

CHRONIC WOUND CARE

Melissa was having frequent blood tests and visits to her kidney doctor, as her kidney function continued to decline. There were periodic adjustments in her medications in order to maintain that delicate balance of various blood readings, and Melissa was beginning to have serious water buildup in her lower legs and feet during the daytime. Blisters formed on her lower legs and they became infected, beginning what became several months of wound care to heal up what would have been a simple recovery for a healthy person.

Due to the excessive water buildup in her legs, the wound care center had to clean the wound, pack it with medications, and wrap her entire lower leg from the knee down to her toes. This wrapping kept the water pressure under control so the wound would heal properly. For several months, I took Melissa to the clinic every seven to ten days to have the wound cleaned up and rewrapped. A few times we tried to do the treatments at home without the wrapping, but it became impossible to keep other blisters from forming and breaking open from the water pressure. Thankfully, this only happened with one leg, and the other one didn't experience any of the open sores. It was a long process, but eventually the original wound healed itself from the inside out and we avoided any additional major wounds for quite some time.

While dealing with this frequent wound care, it became obvious to us that the diuretics alone were not able to deal with the water retention. As Melissa's other blood tests showed serious decline in kidney function, it wasn't long before her doctor recommended she prepare for dialysis. Of course, she was reluctant to start dialysis, but he finally told her, "Well, Melissa, you could choose to do nothing and go home and go to sleep. That would not be a bad way to die."

Melissa didn't care for her doctor's less than comforting assessment, but without dialysis or God's miraculous intervention in raw medical terms, that was the choice she faced. She eventually agreed to attend the training class, where both of us learned about the options for dialysis and many details about how the treatment works. We knew that Melissa's inability to manage very well by herself at home meant her only dialysis option would be outside the home at the outpatient dialysis center.

Preparing for Dialysis

In March of 2006, after several preparatory visits to see the vascular surgeon and after performing ultrasound tests for potential surgery options, Melissa was back in the hospital for two days to have a fistula created in her upper left arm. The fistula is formed by surgically joining a vein to an artery. After a few months, the vein enlarges and matures as the optimal access point for the dialysis needles. If dialysis were needed before the fistula was ready, the doctor would insert a catheter into a neck artery where the dialysis procedure could be performed.

Melissa's blood pressure was running low after this surgery, but she talked the doctors into letting her go home the next day. She was very tired when we got home, and immediately fell asleep in her chair. About an hour later, I tried to wake her up so she could eat something, but I could not wake her. I checked her blood sugar. It looked okay, and she was breathing. But she would not wake up. I called 911 to get the paramedics there immediately. While they were checking her vital signs, she finally started waking up and became adamant that she was not returning to the hospital. The paramedics asked her to sign a release form that said she was refusing transport.

While healing up from the fistula surgery, Melissa was getting additional heart tests on an outpatient basis. Unfortunately, these tests revealed that her heart pumping volume had reduced to a point where she was a candidate for a defibrillator. Melissa now had a high likelihood of experiencing cardiac arrest, so a defibrillator embedded in her upper chest would provide the electric shock needed, under appropriate conditions, to get her heart back into proper rhythm. In June of 2006, she spent two days in the hospital for the surgery to insert a defibrillator device, and the electrical leads running down into her heart. Normally, doctors prefer to put these devices near the heart on the left side, but because of Melissa's fistula on that side, the defibrillator was placed on the right side. This presented a slight increase in risk due to longer electrical leads and potential clotting issues from the fistula.

MORE EMOTIONAL CHALLENGES

The next month, on July 28, 2006, Melissa got a call from her sister Barbara telling her that Melissa's mother, Jo, had passed away. This was emotionally draining for her to handle while dealing with all her health challenges. We knew immediately that she was unable to travel to Kansas City for the funeral, but thankfully, Barbara and family were there to take care of the arrangements. Jo had lived a long life of ninety-three years. In recent years, due to dementia, she was frequently unable to recognize Melissa's voice on the phone. It was no less of a loss for Melissa, though, to have to say good-bye to her mother from a distance.

Barbara told Melissa that while a nurse was moving Jo in her wheelchair into a hospital elevator, Jo had slumped over and passed away. Melissa and I had last visited her mother three years earlier on a trip to her nursing home in Kansas City. During that visit, and ever since, we sought any opportunity we could to appeal to Jo's Catholic faith and remind her to trust in Jesus for her eternal salvation. We prayed that despite her dementia, God was able to keep her heart in his care, and we hoped that she was now in his presence in heaven.

Although I went through all these events with Melissa, it is remarkable to step back and look at the number of health challenges she endured quite well. I guess in some ways we became numb to everything. Melissa's life was reduced to sitting in her chair during the day and doing her best to get to the bathroom in time, something that wasn't always possible. Two or three times each night, I helped Melissa get back into bed, for she could no longer lift her legs onto the bed by herself. We continued to pray for God's strength and Melissa's healing, but it probably isn't too surprising that I had some very difficult days through all of this. I don't believe I was angry at God. Rather, I was trying to focus all that anger on Satan. I was asking *Why?* and *What next?* and wondering how we could possibly get through anything else. I prayed I wasn't angry at Melissa or blaming her for getting us into this situation.

DEALING WITH THE RAGE

During the decline in Melissa's health, I experienced some brief fits of rage, reminiscent of my redheaded temper as a child. Thankfully, with God's help, my rage was contained. On one day in particular, when something about Melissa's health problems set me off, I was so angry, I needed to let off some steam. I left the room where she was at the time and had enough presence of mind to let out my frustration on a small stuffed animal I took from a shelf. I hurled it across the room into a wall.

Unfortunately, I had forgotten that this stuffed animal was a battery-operated singing hamster that I had given to Melissa for a previous Valentine's Day gift. This meant that the hamster weighed a few more ounces than I realized, and so a hard, plastic base on the critter left a small divot in the wall. Although I later patched the damage, I could still see the mark as a constant reminder of my shame for expressing my anger as I had done. Fortunately, the hamster survived and can still sing a peppy rendition of "I Think I Love You."

> But now you must rid yourselves of all such things as these: anger, rage, malice, slander, and filthy language from your lips.
> (Colossians 3:8)

Although Melissa had agreed to the dialysis training class and had completed the fistula surgery, she still was putting off dialysis treatment. She declared defiantly, "I'll start when I'm ready."

Her kidney doctor believed she needed to start immediately. We were told that the longer she waited, and the longer her body continued to weaken, Melissa would have more difficulty adjusting to the dialysis treatment and associated side effects. I also knew from some Internet research that the dialysis treatment itself carried risks for infections—although people can live for many years on dialysis.

For most dialysis patients, the only problem is with their kidneys. Melissa, however, was faced with a long list of health issues stemming from her battle with diabetes. Giving her advice on when to start dialysis was a difficult thing to do. If I strongly advocated she start immediately, she could experience an infection or other complication that would make things worse. On the other hand, if I told her to put it off a little longer, this non-action would decrease her long-term survival rate based on statistics alone. Without God's intervention, beyond what the doctors were able to do, it was clear she needed to start dialysis very soon.

STARTING DIALYSIS

Melissa cut a deal with her kidney doctor in August of 2006 to start outpatient dialysis after Labor Day. However, her body couldn't wait that long. About a week before that date, she began acting very strangely.

"Melissa, did you just feel your hand twitch? I saw it move," I asked her one evening as we were watching television together.

"Yes, I felt it. It has been doing that for a few days in my hands and legs."

"Why didn't you tell me? This might be something serious. We'd better call your doctor."

Melissa discounted the muscle twitching, but said she would call her doctor the next day to ask about it. An hour or so later that evening, some more pronounced symptoms appeared. Melissa was getting up out of her chair so she could use her walker to go to the bathroom.

"Where's the bathroom? Do I go this way to the left, or is it over there?" Melissa asked me, as if she wasn't in her own home.

"What do you mean? You know where the bathroom is," I replied as I guided her in the correct direction.

"Oh, that's right, now I remember. Who are you?"

"Melissa, it's me, your husband, Jim. Don't you know who I am?"

"Jim . . . right . . . I know . . . you're my husband."

Melissa needed to get to the hospital immediately. After a few minutes of discussion, I convinced her it was time to call the ambulance. We gathered up a bag of things to take to the hospital and I called 911.

When the doctor evaluated Melissa in the emergency room, he confirmed that she could not have waited much longer before her body would have succumbed to the dangerous levels of toxins in her blood. She was given daily dialysis sessions over the next several days to get her system cleaned out. When the dialysis nurses attempted to use Melissa's fistula for the first time, they had some problems, and she ended up with massive bruising on her upper left arm. Instead, they inserted a catheter into her neck and used that for dialysis. The advantage of the perm-cath was that the nurses could stick the needles into the perm-cath ports instead of Melissa's arm. The catheter approach, however, does carry more risk of infection, and the blood flow rate is lower than a fully mature fistula. After about a week in the hospital, Melissa was moved to a sub-acute health care center for another few weeks. The staff provided her wheelchair transportation to outpatient dialysis three times a week.

Melissa was highly motivated to take advantage of the therapy sessions at the health care center when she first arrived. She needed to build up the strength in her legs so she could function at home by herself again. When she had her first session with the therapist, she set a goal for herself to be able to visit her best friend's house, where she had to go up a couple steps. Melissa hadn't been able to walk up a single step for a year or more. After a couple weeks, though, she lowered her expectations to simply wanting to get home as soon as she could. The staff was at first reluctant to release her, but we felt that in many ways, she would do better in her familiar surroundings.

At home, Melissa could use her reclining lift-chair during the day and get to and from the bathroom on her own. In this health care center, she took all her meals in the room because it had become too painful for her to sit in her wheelchair for long periods of time in the lunchroom. This meant she was spending too much time in the hospital bed. I made some added preparations around the house in anticipation of her return. I installed some handrails in the shower and placed a portable toilet with handrails over the regular toilet.

When Melissa finally made it home, after three weeks in the health care center, we started the weekly regimen of getting her to dialysis three times a week on our own. We got up at 3:00 A.M. on dialysis days so I could drive her to the center by 5:00 A.M., go to the office for a few hours, get her back home after dialysis, and then return to the office to finish out my workday. As long as Melissa was able to stand on her own, this schedule worked out.

About a month later, in mid-October, Melissa woke up with severe knee pain and was unable to stand. Once again, I had to call the paramedics to get her to the hospital. She spent about a week there, and the doctors never figured out why she couldn't stand up that day. After some rest and therapy, she was back home again.

When Colorado Springs experienced the first blizzard of the winter 2006–2007 season, Melissa and I learned that skipping dialysis for one session is sometimes a wise choice. The snow was coming down heavily and piling up while she was in her dialysis session in late October. When we got into the van to drive home, it quickly became evident that this was the worst storm we had ever driven in. Normally, we never ventured out in weather as bad as this, or anything as close to as bad as this. We had to take some detours on our way home when certain roads became impassible. We drove through total whiteout conditions for the last few blocks before reaching our street.

When I pulled onto our less-traveled street, I soon was stuck in the deep snow—one block from our house. For Melissa, this might as well have been a million miles. I couldn't get her back home by myself. A generous neighbor helped me get her out of the van and into her ambulatory chair. We dragged her chair a few yards in deep snow over to his four-wheel drive vehicle and then pushed Melissa up into the truck cab for the short trip to our house. After busting through a four-foot snowdrift in front of our garage, we were home.

In early November, Melissa had the catheter removed from her neck and she now had to deal with the dialysis needles in her arm for each treatment. Some days, the technicians were able to get the needles in on the first attempt, but at other times they struggled and caused more bruising on her arm. On more than one occasion, when Melissa was leaving the dialysis center, she declared she wasn't coming back anymore. I would let those feelings pass without comment. By the next appointment, she was ready to go without complaint. At these times, I would think, *If it were me, I'm not sure I would be willing to endure everything Melissa is going through.*

One day, after attending a meeting at work for several hours, I called Melissa to let her know I was on my way home. The phone rang, but she didn't answer. After several rings, the answering machine picked up, at which point I became very concerned. A few times in the previous weeks, Melissa had left the phone off the hook and all I could get was a busy signal. Because the answering machine came on this time, I knew Melissa couldn't get to the phone. I prayed that she had gone to the bathroom and forgotten to take the phone with her, but I feared something more serious. All I could do was get home as quickly as I could and pray along the way that Melissa was okay.

When I entered the house, I found her on the floor in the kitchen. The oven door was open, and a casserole dish was slightly askew on the upper rack. "What happened, Melissa—are you okay?" I asked, kneeling next to her to see if she was hurt.

With an apparent feeling of embarrassment, but surprisingly calm, Melissa explained, "I was trying to get the casserole into the oven and I lost my balance."

Anger welled up in my voice. "Didn't I specifically tell you before I went to work not to do that?"

"Yes, you did. I heard the phone ring," she said timidly. "I couldn't reach it. All I could do was wait until you got home."

I let out a large sigh of exasperation. "How long have you been here on the floor?"

"For two or three hours, I guess."

The thought upset me intensely that as I had sat for hours in a meeting, my wife was lying on the floor at home, helpless.

Again, I called the paramedics and they got Melissa off the floor and back into her chair. Before the paramedics left the house, they recommended we get a medical alert device installed, so Melissa could call for help without having the phone within reach. Although she didn't want me to bother with it, I looked into getting such a device connected to our existing alarm system.

Melissa was very sore from having been on the floor so long, but we didn't realize at the time how serious that can be for a diabetes patient. The long compression of one spot can lead to the skin dying from poor circulation and result in underlying infections that go unnoticed for days or weeks.

Although Melissa was having some home therapy sessions, and had progressed to a rolling walker that made it easier to get around the house, she wasn't making sufficient progress because she was too weak to move around much during the day. That she was sitting in a chair all day or lying in bed at night meant she was more prone to develop pressure sores on her hips and legs.

Melissa had been complaining of her hip hurting each time we went to dialysis. Closing the van door against her right side was causing intense pain. We started noticing a small sore at that location and attempted to treat it at home by ourselves. I soon suggested she get an appointment for the wound clinic again, but she insisted I keep cleaning the growing wound myself. While treating the wound, we also noticed the formation of dark scabs on her upper legs. At the time we didn't realize that this was dead skin caused by poor circulation.

Leaving Home for the Last Time

On November 27, 2006, Melissa slipped out of her lift-chair in the living room. She lay there on the floor for a couple hours until I got home from work. I called 911 for an assist. After Melissa was back in her chair, she insisted we stay at home even though the paramedics and I were trying to convince her to go to the hospital. She just wasn't going. As I let her sleep in the chair a while, I set up an appointment with our home alarm company to get a medic-alert device added to our system as soon as possible. At the same time, I was beginning to admit to myself that we had reached our limit for what we could do with Melissa at home. I believe we were both in denial that she couldn't be at home by herself anymore.

I woke Melissa so we could get her to the bathroom and into bed. It took more than thirty minutes before I could accomplish the task. She barely had the strength to make it to the bathroom, and when she reached the bed, she collapsed immediately and went to sleep. The next day was a scheduled dialysis session and I knew that if she didn't get on her feet in the morning, I would have to call the paramedics to get her to the hospital. I lay down next to Melissa in the bed and prayed. Through tears, I asked God to be merciful to her. Although I didn't say these words out loud, God knew, and I knew, what I meant. I was praying that the Lord would take her home. No more dialysis, no more hospitals, no more calls to 911, no more pain. By midnight, Melissa woke up and agreed she needed to go to the hospital for her dialysis treatment. This was the last time my wife was in our home.

At the hospital, the doctors quickly confirmed there were serious infections in the wound we had been treating at home. They also found that the dark skin on her upper legs was dead tissue covering additional infections. Minor surgery was needed for debridement or removal of the dead tissue in the infected wounds. In addition to intensive antibiotic treatments, the doctors used vacuum pumps to keep the wounds clear of fluid as they healed from the inside out. Melissa was put into a room by herself for isolation, and the staff and I had to use gloves and gowns when having contact with her.

After a week at the main hospital, Melissa was transferred to a long-term-care hospital to continue treatment for the infected wounds. There, Melissa received dialysis treatments at her bedside. Over the next several weeks, she endured even more pain each time the wound dressings had to be changed. In addition to the major wounds, annoying sores on her right heel and toes worsened and became more painful, so painful that Melissa was unable to put any weight on that foot. This foot wound prevented her from getting out of the bed for two-and-a-half months, which led to further weakening of her legs, despite attempts to provide therapy while she was bedridden.

By this time, Melissa's fistula in her arm was not working well enough, so once again a perm-cath had to be inserted for dialysis access. This made it easier, but again it increased her risk of infection. Although Melissa was in a special room where everyone used gloves, gowns, and masks as appropriate, the fact that her body was already combating infections in the wound sites meant the infections could spread throughout her body.

Confusion Sets In

Melissa had good days and bad days. The pain medications and long hospital stay led her to develop confused thinking and hallucinations. The hallucinations were not without some humor, such as the night she called 911 when she thought she needed to be rescued from the hospital staff. After she called 911, she called me at home at about 3:00 A.M. She said the nurses had moved her to some other room and I needed to come down there right away and pick her up.

This confusion made it impractical for Melissa to make any phone calls or pick up the phone when I tried to reach her from home. She repeatedly got the phone mixed up with the nurse call button. She also began seeing bugs in her bed and got very animated trying to get them off the sheets. The doctors and I didn't see any bugs, so we tried to reason with her that these were hallucinations. I tried to humor her by using a stuffed bear or stuffed dog to "eat the bugs," and actually that seemed to put her at ease for a while.

On some days, the confusion caused Melissa to think she could get up out of the bed and go home. She became restless, started pulling off the sheets, and tried to get out of bed by herself. A few times the nurses came close to using hand restraints to keep her from hurting herself. One evening, I arrived for a visit to find Melissa's oxygen tube pulled off her nose, the sheets and a pillow on the floor, her hospital gown almost off entirely, and a partly eaten sandwich and paper plate strewn all over the bed. I was upset that the nurses allowed this to happen, but then I quickly realized Melissa could have done all of this in a few minutes' time between staff visits. When I left the room to go home that night, she yelled out to the nurses in the hallway. It was the most heartbreaking departure I had to make. I kept walking down the hallway ignoring my wife's voice. That night the nurses gave Melissa a light sedative for her own safety.

The medical staff's inability to know precisely how much pain medication remained in Melissa's blood system after each dialysis session led to a respiratory arrest. The nursing staff had to administer CPR to get her heart back into proper rhythm. As a result of this event, the physicians had to reduce her use of certain medications, which added to her daily pain, but which gradually reduced some of the mental confusion. The alternating pain and numbness was also increasing in her left hand, due to the reduced blood flow caused by the fistula in her left arm. This condition caused an increase in various spots of dead skin on her left hand. Although we didn't talk about it, I could see that Melissa was in danger of losing at least a portion of one or two fingers as the necrotic tissue spread.

CHAPTER 10

A Secret Revealed

Christmas is supposed to be a time of joy and celebration. As Melissa's health had been declining over the years, I tended to be the Scrooge of our marriage and not always as excited as I was in my childhood about putting up a Christmas tree. In 2006, however, I put up the tree and all the decorations for Melissa to enjoy over Thanksgiving—just a few days before she entered the hospital.

Despite Melissa being bedridden since Thanksgiving, we maintained some normality by remembering special occasions in the month of December. We celebrated her fifty-first birthday on December 6, and Christmas three weeks later. On Christmas Eve and Christmas Day, a small group of singers and musicians made the rounds of the hospital rooms, doing their best to cheer up the patients and visiting family members. The hospital chaplain also made visits to Melissa's room during the holiday period. It was comforting to share our faith with the chaplain, who understood the health challenges Melissa was experiencing.

The nursing staff helped us make the best of these trying times in the hospital during the holidays. They came to

---

appreciate Melissa's sense of humor, which she still displayed in the midst of all her discomfort. The hallucinations and confusion made her humor even more pronounced as we all laughed with Melissa in many situations.

CHRISTMAS EVE PHONE CALL

One of the Christmas Eve traditions Melissa and I had shared most of our years away from home was a phone call to the family gathered in St. Louis. This would be an especially meaningful call this year, given Melissa's serious health issues and the grim reality of her long-term prognosis. At the appointed time on Christmas Eve, I called my parents. Everyone at the other end was taking turns talking, and they passed the phone around the room. Melissa talked briefly, but because of her somewhat confused condition, I ended up doing most of the talking for both of us. I struggled to hold back the emotion rising within me, as I became more aware of the overwhelming reality of what our lives had become. Eventually, my sister-in-law Norma got on the line, and we began talking about an idea Melissa had been suggesting the previous few days.

"Jim, I don't know if Melissa told you this yet, but she asked me to come to Colorado to be with both of you at the hospital."

"Yes, she did talk to me about you coming up here, but I didn't realize she managed to ask you about it on the phone."

"I could drive up there and spend time with Melissa while you take a break."

"Norma, what if your car broke down on the way or we had a snowstorm come through and you got stranded? Then I'd have to get you rescued while I'm trying to be here with Melissa."

As we went back and forth on this topic for several minutes, I found myself repeating the same thing several times.

"Norma, I have enough going on up here. I don't need anyone else to take care of. Please, please, stop. I don't want you to come up here right now."

I'd reached my limit. It was pointless to talk about this anymore. Surprising myself as well as Norma, I hung up the phone.

Immediately, I regretted what I'd done. What a Christmas this had become. I was clearly losing it, and I couldn't face the fact that my wife's condition was taking a toll on my emotions and my spirit. I got my sister Sue back on the phone.

"Sue, I'm so sorry, I just hung up on Norma. I can't imagine how I could keep up with everything I'm already doing as well as having Norma around here. It just wouldn't work out."

My anger with Norma now turned to tears, as I couldn't hold back the flood of emotions pouring out of my spirit. Although it was my own sister, I felt embarrassed by my actions, and now I was allowing myself to lose further control.

Why was Melissa so insistent on having Norma come to visit her in the hospital?

In just a few days, I would understand why.

THE BIG REVELATION

On Saturday, December 30, 2006, I was talking with Melissa at her bedside before her dinner tray arrived.

"I have something I need to tell you, Jim."

Despite the hallucinations, I sensed this was something serious and real.

"Since I've been in this hospital so long, I've been praying and getting myself right with God."

I was glad to hear her say this, although coming from someone who had been serving God for many years, it sounded out of place. I thought this might be due to her confused thinking. Melissa never enjoyed talking about how it would be in heaven, or anything else related to death, and I didn't want to stress the topic of heaven, out of concern she might think I was looking forward to her dying. It was more important, however, that she be assured of her eternal life, so I decided to convince myself she understood what she was saying.

"That's good, Melissa, I'm glad you are being sure of your salvation. You do remember that you accepted Jesus as your Savior and that you will be with him in heaven some day, right?"

"Yes, I know that." Melissa then made two statements that didn't make any sense to me initially: "Reed Branstetter is my dad and I lived on Benton Boulevard."

I repeated her words back to her to be certain I heard them correctly. "You said Reed Branstetter is your dad and you lived on Benton?"

As she acknowledged her words, I knew this was not a hallucination. I typed the information into my cell phone notepad as quickly as I could. I wasn't sure at the moment, but I believed Melissa was sharing some details about her past that I had never known.

These first two facts were not significant to me, but what she said next confirmed that this was a life-changing confession.

"Dennis, Suzan, and David are my children, and Ray was my husband. He's not my brother."

This was another one of those moments when my mind was racing. I was trying to decide what to say next. Knowing that we had celebrated Melissa's fifty-first birthday earlier in the month, I asked her, "So when were you born?"

"I was born on December 6, 1938."

I paused, and with difficulty, I slowly repeated what she had just told me. "You were born in 1938? That makes you about seventeen years older than I am."

"Yes, I guess so."

As my mind was trying to process this incredible information, the Lord enabled me to recognize the significance of this moment. I measured my words carefully. This confession meant that the first picture I had of "Melissa Jo Carrington" in 1976 never was Melissa, and that whole ʻdeception with the mono was a cover-up for the real deception that was now being revealed to me one fact at a time. At this moment in the hospital room, I don't believe I had any anger. I was more focused on understanding what Melissa wanted to share with me. I didn't want to risk interrupting her thought process in her delicate condition.

Melissa made these astonishing statements in what seemed to be a matter-of-fact tone. The medications and her poor physical condition contributed to her subdued attitude. To me she was like a little child caught with her hand in a cookie jar. She knew she was guilty and no longer needed to hide the truth. Melissa probably was feeling a tremendous relief, being able to talk to me about this for the first time in thirty-one years.

Melissa's next statement captured the fear and tremendous burden she had carried for so many years, "I wanted to tell you before, but I thought you would leave me."

COMMITMENT TO OUR MARRIAGE

I assured Melissa of my commitment to her and to our marriage. "I love you, Melissa, I forgive you, and I'm not going to leave you." I also admitted, "But you have to know that this is quite a shock to me because I had no idea in all these years about any of this. If you had told me this when we first started talking on the phone, it would have been too much to handle as a nineteen year old."

Melissa must have known this likelihood from the start. After hearing this full confession, I believed it was out of love that she had created this deception in the first place. Perhaps my initial belief that her actions were out of love was some sort of self-defense mechanism to mask the more difficult realization that would come to me later. The longer she maintained the deception, the harder it became to reveal the truth. I believe that if she had told me this secret at the one year or five year or even ten year point in our marriage, I would have been as committed to our relationship—although my initial reaction may have been different. At this difficult point in our lives, with Melissa lying in a hospital bed, my heart went out to her as I imagined how complex it was to maintain this lie. I wondered if deceiving me and my family all these years was a contributing cause for her medical problems.

Was Melissa preparing to reveal this secret to me at Christmas time when she was asking Norma to drive up from St. Louis? Was she afraid of how I might react to the news if I was here by myself? As I pondered these thoughts, Melissa and I exchanged questions and answers about various facts while I continued making notes and forcing myself to accept what was happening.

"Melissa, what about your sister Barbara. When did you first meet her?"

"Well, I wasn't adopted in the way I told you before we were married, and I didn't grow up in Chalmette, as I always told you."

"You weren't adopted? So is Barbara really your sister?"

"She's my half-sister. Barbara and I grew up together in Kansas City, but she was born about seven years after I was."

"So you grew up right near Richards-Gebaur, where we first met?" I was trying to make it all register in my mind.

"Reed Branstetter was Barbara's father, but my stepfather. My name growing up was Charlene Frances Branstetter. So,

I guess I was adopted, but not by my mother, as I made you believe all these years. Josephine was my real mother."

"Charlene Frances." The same first and middle names that were on Melissa's social security card. It was right there in front of me the whole time. Melissa said she never would have revealed any of this to me if her mother Josephine had not passed away the previous summer. I wondered if her mother and family were a part of this deception.

WHO ELSE KNEW?

I continued my questioning. "Who else knew about this? Were the kids, Barbara, or your mom all part of this?"

"No. Nobody in my family knew I was making up these stories or lying to you and your family."

I realized that this would have been possible, because Melissa always told me to call her Charlene around her family, which of course was her birth name. Her family never made a habit of reminiscing about the past when they were together. As hard as it was to believe, at no time did any of Melissa's family unknowingly say anything that would have blown her cover. I'm sure there must have been many little things said here and there that, were I to hear again, in light of this revelation, I would now have a different interpretation. With the filter of what I thought was the truth, I discounted anything that didn't fit with the facts as I knew them.

Melissa called each of her children—Dennis, Suzan, and David—to let them know what she had confessed to me. She explained that she was telling me the truth about being their mother. I overheard part of Suzan's reply on the phone when she said, "It's about time." As I later learned from Suzan, she was indicating that it was about time her mother acknowledged Suzan as her daughter. According to Suzan, during a visit to our home early in our marriage, Melissa's deception forced her to introduce Suzan as her niece to our neighbor.

Melissa muttered under her breath at that time, "Don't say a word. I'll explain later."

Melissa never explained, and Suzan suffered the effects of this denial by her mother in the years that followed. Suzan never knew that I was being deceived. Likewise, Dennis and David said they didn't have any idea that their mother was keeping me from the truth. Both of them respected me as their stepfather and, as unbelievable as this sounds, they never realized I didn't know they were Melissa's sons.

I decided to leave the hospital room earlier than usual that evening for obvious reasons. "Melissa, I'm going to head home early tonight. I need some time at home to think through all this. We can talk more tomorrow."

"I understand. I'll see you tomorrow. I love you."

"I love you, too."

Discovering the Melissa I Never Knew

When I arrived at home, I immediately went to a box of old pictures in the basement. These pictures now took on new meaning. When I looked at some of these pictures previously, they had confused me. The apparent timeframe just wasn't right for any of these to be pictures of Melissa. The family photos in this collection only showed two girls, and none of her eleven brothers anywhere, but I had noticed that one of the girls was Melissa's sister, Barbara. I had just chalked it up to another part of the mystery of Melissa's mystifying family and left the pictures in the box where I found them.

I believed Melissa and Barbara were separated at birth, so I didn't expect to see any pictures with the two of them together as children. The two girls I saw in these pictures didn't have similar body types or facial characteristics. I discounted the relationship as some other relative or a friend of Barbara's. It was now dawning on me that most of what I knew about Melissa wasn't true, and I had to start from the beginning to figure out who she really was. This box of at least two hundred family pictures from the early 1900s up to the 1960s held the key to her past. I saw pictures of Melissa as a baby in 1938 and a much later picture with her son Dennis in her lap in the late 1950s.

Alone in our home, some emotions of anger welled up within me. Although I had expressed my love and forgiveness to Melissa in the hospital, I felt hurt about what she confessed to me, and I expressed my feelings out loud to God. I suppose I was experiencing some shock as I tried to re-examine the events of our lives in light of this disturbing discovery. I found it hard to believe she could have kept such a secret all these years. I began wondering if deep in my heart I knew about Melissa's age and children but was subconsciously denying it to myself.

I did something that night and the first few days afterward that proved to me I really had no idea throughout our marriage about my wife's actual age. I got out the picture of "Melissa" that I had first received from her in the mail in 1976, and I compared it with several of the pictures of Charlene I now had in front of me. I even did some simple facial recognition measurements to see if there was any possibility the original picture was of Melissa. I was clinging to the faint hope that this picture from 1976 was a picture of the woman I had shared my life with for the past thirty years.

As I continued to study photo after photo from the 1940s and 1950s, I questioned the reality of it all in my mind and continually asked myself if there was any way this could possibly *not* be true. *Could this be a relative who looks like Melissa?*

When I found a large high school picture of Charlene in this collection, I discovered something that clinched it for me.

As I had known for years, Melissa's left iris was slower to react to flash photography than her right iris. I looked closely at that high school picture taken in 1955, the year before I was born. I focused in on her two blue eyes and was drawn to the different appearance of her left eye. There was no mistaking it. The left eye with the larger pupil stood out as undeniable evidence that Melissa Jo Carrington was in fact Charlene Frances Branstetter.

I spent a couple hours that night going through all the pictures and soaking in the truth of Melissa's life that I had never known. I began remembering the many red flags I had seen throughout our marriage. There were so many questions that had gone unanswered, until now. No wonder I couldn't e-file our income taxes, because the automated process was able to catch the mismatch between Melissa's birth date on the income tax form and the actual birth date attached to that social security number. No wonder Melissa insisted over the years that she be the first one to go through the mail. There was no telling what incriminating pieces of mail might have shown up—or did show up. I also remembered that Melissa never received those annual social security statements on her birth date, as I received each year. Or at least if she was receiving them, I never saw them. I just assumed her earnings when we first got married weren't enough to trigger this annual statement.

As I rehearsed these red flags and unanswered questions in my mind, I began to realize that my middle-child traits of compromise and peacemaking had led me to be an enabler of Melissa's deception. Although I may have been a naive nineteen year old when this started, I clearly allowed Melissa to keep up her deception by not insisting on answers. Demonstrating a forgiving and kind heart does not mean I should have facilitated her secrecy and allowed behavior in her life that I would find unthinkable in my own.

Over the next few days, as Melissa and I went through the New Year's holiday into 2007, we spent much time talking about the facts of her real life growing up as Charlene. I had to initiate the questions slowly, as I could see that it wasn't easy for her to start sharing the details of her autobiography. After so many years of maintaining an alternate life story, and still dealing with periodic confusion and hallucinations, she had to concentrate very hard to separate truth from deception. Melissa never could answer the most perplexing question.

"Melissa, who was this younger woman in the photographs you sent me before we ever met?"

"I don't know."

I asked that question several times in the coming weeks, but Melissa never was able to explain how things started when she first saw my picture. I could only speculate on what involvement Robbie or other friends might have had in getting us together initially.

One day during this gradual debriefing process, Melissa suggested I look in the "top drawer" at home for some papers. When I returned home, I looked in the top drawer of her dresser and found nothing unusual. I looked in all the drawers of her desk and again found nothing. Finally, I looked in the top drawer of her filing cabinet and discovered one of those annual earnings statements from the Social Security Administration, hidden beneath the hanging folders. I slowly opened the envelope and saw the name, "Melissajo C. Marr." The birth date was December 6, 1938. The earnings statement showed that Melissa had two dollars of taxable earnings in 1953. I was familiar with the latter portion of the statement that showed her earnings history since we were married.

Any brief feelings of anger against Melissa were soon replaced with deepening sympathy for what she had been going through, and what she was going through now. As we continued to piece together more facts, it dawned on me that I had a major task ahead of me to get her official records updated with her correct age. I also needed to get her enrolled for her social security and Medicare benefits, for she actually was sixty-eight years old instead of fifty-one, as I had believed. I had to start by finding her birth certificate.

I began talking with Melissa's sister Barbara over the phone and writing numerous e-mails. For years, Barbara had been doing extensive research on her family tree. A few months before, she had e-mailed Melissa and me several yearbook pictures she found with Josephine and Reed. The pictures also included some references to a young man named Charles Lammons, whom Barbara now revealed was Melissa's birth father.

When Melissa and I originally received those high school pictures from Barbara, I was confused about what all the relationships were supposed to be. Melissa's fabricated life story just did not fit with those high school pictures. I figured Barbara was giving Melissa some insight into their shared birth family, while also showing that her birth family had some contact with her adoptive mother, Josephine, back in high school. Now that I knew the truth, I realized that Barbara had sent us pictures of Melissa's mother and stepfather with whom Melissa and she had shared their lives as children. Unfortunately, at the time we received those old yearbook photos, Melissa couldn't acknowledge the significance of Barbara's discoveries.

With Barbara's help in quickly confirming that Melissa was born in Kansas City as Charlene Frances Lammons, to Charles Lammons and Josephine Castillo, it became quite easy to order a Missouri birth certificate via the Internet. I had several certified copies of Melissa's birth certificate in my hands within days of her revelation to me about her actual age. After I learned that her birth father was Charles Lammons, Melissa kept telling me about something else being in a top drawer at home. When I got back home, I checked the top drawer of Melissa's bedside table that I had failed to check on my previous search. Hidden under a piece of brown paper that was lining the drawer, I found a certificate of baptism from a Catholic church in Los Angeles.

Melissa had spent some years in California during World War II, when her stepfather, Reed, was in Europe. Some of Josephine's relatives lived around Los Angeles, so Melissa had attended a Catholic school in that area while her stepfather was serving overseas. The certificate I found at home said that Charlene Frances Branstetter was the child of Reed Branstetter and Josephine Castillo, and she was born in Los Angeles on December 6, 1938. This church certificate contradicted the state birth records from Missouri.

Although the baptism certificate was an original and dated 1957—for a baptism that occurred on November 5, 1944— the information Josephine had provided to this church was not true. She and Reed provided this false information, and the church was only providing documentation of what was in their records from thirteen years earlier. The saying "Like mother, like daughter" came to mind. It appeared this was similar to what Melissa had done years later in 1976 to provide her proof of birth using a church baptism certificate. The key difference was that the latter certificate was totally fabricated.

TRYING TO PROVE IT

Although I now had Charlene's birth certificate, I didn't have enough proof to show that Charlene Frances Branstetter was in fact Melissa Jo Marr, as it appeared on Melissa's Colorado and Air Force dependent identification cards. I had pictures, grade school records, and graduation announcements to verify that Charlene's high school graduation was in 1955. Visually, this was the same person as Melissa. Unfortunately, it was not good enough for the Colorado Department of Motor Vehicles,

and they would not update her identification card. I was beginning to think I needed a lawyer to obtain a judge's ruling that
Charlene and Melissa were the same person.

To get more legal documentation, Melissa called her former
husband, Ray, to help her remember their wedding and divorce
dates and locations. Within a few weeks, I was holding the
official documents for those two events as well. Melissa married
Ray at the age of seventeen on May 12, 1956, in Gatesville,
Texas, where Ray was stationed in the Army. They were
divorced on April 17, 1968, in Lenexa, Kansas.

I was getting closer to having enough proof, but I needed
more. The best evidence came in the form of a certified letter
that the Social Security Administration provided when I went
to enroll Melissa for benefits. They printed out the name history
on her social security number from 1952 to the present. In
1952, Melissa had initially requested the social security number
using the name Charlene Frances Branstetter. It is not clear if
Melissa was ever formally adopted by Reed Branstetter, but she
was using that last name in all her early school records.

It was fascinating to see how Melissa had reported her father's
name upon each name change. At first, she listed her father as
Reed Branstetter. In 1956, Melissa updated her name on her
social security records to use her husband, Ray's, last name,
while still showing Reed as her father. But in 1977, Melissa
changed her name to Charlene Marr, and listed her father as
Charles Lammons. She made her final name change in 1988 to
Melissajo Charlene Marr, but her social security card showed
her name as "Melissa Jo C. Marr." I had never known that
the "C" on her social security card stood for "Charlene." I had
always assumed it represented her supposed maiden name,
"Carrington." On this name change, Melissa listed her father
as unknown.

Was Melissa conflicted about who her father really was? I
thought to myself as I read this amazing progression of names.

Perhaps for the final name change in 1988, she thought it best to avoid listing a father's name at all. She told me in the hospital that as a young child she remembered being called by the last name Lammons, which of course didn't match her stepfather's name. Apparently, Josephine and Reed either informally or formally changed her last name to Branstetter. This name change had helped Charlene avoid the teasing from other kids in the neighborhood about her name being different.

I gave up on the Colorado Department of Motor Vehicles when, on my second visit, with enough evidence now in my hands for them to approve an update, they told me that Melissa would have to be present in person to get a new identification card. Fortunately, the Air Force Academy personnel office was accustomed to handling cases where military deployments made it impossible to get identification cards updated for family dependents. They said I could use a notarized photo and then they would take a "picture of a picture" to put on the identification card. As soon as I got a letter from Medicare indicating that Melissa's enrollment was pending completion, and she was assigned an interim Medicare account number, the Academy was able to make Melissa's new dependent identification card with her corrected age. This occurred on the fifth of February, nine days before her cardiac arrest.

While I was working on updating Melissa's identification card, I was also building a long list of doctors and other organizations where knowing Melissa's true age was critical. For them, my word and the birth certificate was sufficient evidence to update her age. I made personal visits to those offices in and within reach of Colorado Springs. To the others, I mailed out birth certificates or made phone calls to get her records corrected. One of those phone calls was to the office within the Social Security Administration that handled Medicare enrollments for dialysis patients.

When I had believed Melissa's age was only fifty, at the time she started dialysis, she was required to initiate Medicare paperwork for dialysis coverage, not to authenticate her age. On that paperwork, we entered her birth year as 1955. The person I talked to, while trying to get her records updated, said that the date we wrote on the form apparently was ignored by a clerk when they processed the dialysis paperwork. They must have entered the social security number and taken the birth date off those existing records in the computer. Otherwise, this should have triggered the discovery of Melissa's actual age back in August 2006. But as it turned out, no one even noticed.

More Discoveries

While I was working through these record updates day by day and week by week, Melissa and I continued to discuss more about her past growing up. I compiled more facts to piece together a better understanding of what had happened in her life from the years 1938 to 1976. One weekend, while talking about her birth father, Charles Lammons, she mentioned that there were some pictures of him in that box at home, telling me to look for a Navy uniform. She never met him in person, and only once reached him on the phone sometime during her marriage to Ray. Charles denied being her father. When I got home and searched through the box, I found a few pictures of a Navy enlisted man. One of the pictures had this text written on the back:

> Long Beach, Cal., March 22, 1936
>
> Just thinking——always of you*!
>
> Yours, Carlitos x

I didn't know if "Carlitos" was in fact Charles. I scanned the pictures and e-mailed them to Melissa's sister. Barbara said she hadn't seen them before, but she decided to e-mail them to their cousin in California, who was known as "Little Charles." The next day while I was at the hospital with Melissa, I received an e-mail from Barbara through my cell phone and learned that Little Charles had several pictures he thought Barbara already had. Little Charles had these other pictures because his dad, "Big Charles," was a friend of Charles Lammons while they were in the Navy. I viewed the pictures attached to the e-mail on my cell phone, right at Melissa's bedside. I discovered they included some very touching photos of Charles and Melissa's mother, Josephine.

For the first time in her life, Melissa was seeing photographs of her mother and father together in 1937, in San Diego. The earlier picture I found that was signed Carlitos was Charles, and that note had been written to Josephine. These pictures showed there had been a relationship between Charles and Jo the year before Melissa was born as Charlene Frances Lammons in Kansas City. Jo's marriage certificate to Reed Branstetter in 1942 showed her maiden name as "Josephine Lammons," although neither Barbara nor I have any evidence that she ever married Charles Lammons.

MY TWO STEPSONS

Within the first week of Melissa's revelation, Dennis, his stepson David (who was called "Little David"), and David drove down from Rawlins, Wyoming, to visit with their mother and me. I had previously sent out an e-mail to Melissa's children expressing my sorrow in not knowing all these years that they were her children. I apologized if I had appeared at arm's length during those years, but given how tightly Melissa had controlled my interaction with her family, it was amazing that I was able to form such good relationships with the few family members I had met.

It was a brief but very timely visit with Dennis, David, and Little David on a Sunday afternoon. The day they arrived at the hospital was David's birthday, an appropriate day for him to be with his mother. It gave Dennis, David, and me time to discuss what I was learning from Melissa, and the opportunity to share things with them they had never known about their mother. Melissa had never told them anything about her birth father or any other details from her childhood.

During our few hours together on that Sunday afternoon, with all of us gathered around her bedside, Melissa began talking to Dennis and David about an unsettling topic.

"Dennis, David . . . I want you to decide what things around our house you might want to take home when I'm gone."

"No, we don't need to be doing that today. You're going to be around a lot longer," David said, and Dennis and I were quick to agree.

That was the first time Melissa had ever initiated such discussions about dying. Although it would be prudent to have her express such desires at some point, this day was not that point. We quickly changed the topic of our conversation. Her actions that day did make it easier for me to discuss such matters with her a few weeks later. Having some notes of her wishes would provide me some peace of mind if I ever had to deal with the unthinkable.

Melissa had another humorous flare-up of her hallucinations during this visit with her two sons. Perhaps being with her children was bringing back vivid memories that were getting mixed up with reality. Melissa claimed to be pregnant, and she even got David's wife, Tammy, on the phone from Rawlins to see if she and David would be willing to raise the child in their home.

Fortunately, for most of the time we all visited together, Melissa was well aware of what was going on. At one point, the reality of it all hit her at once, and she began crying. We did our best to comfort her and one another.

THIRTIETH WEDDING ANNIVERSARY

After this visit with her two sons, Melissa and I had the opportunity to celebrate an important milestone in our lives—our thirtieth wedding anniversary. Her best friend bought her a nightgown and Melissa asked the staff for approval to have a special meal brought into the hospital. I created a collage of some pictures of the two of us as children and later in our marriage. I also picked up some flowers and an anniversary card.

Because this was our thirtieth anniversary, I bought Melissa some pearls—the traditional gift for thirty years of marriage. It probably was the fastest anybody had ever purchased a necklace of real pearls. On the way to celebrate at the hospital, I stopped at a jewelry store, looked at a few different strands of pearls, and within a few minutes said, "I'll take this one." The salesperson wrapped up the box of pearls and I was on my way out the door.

I brought in some donuts for the staff to enjoy during the day as they celebrated with us. As dinnertime approached, the hospital staff agreed that Melissa could skip the usual meal that night. Instead, I went out to get some Red Lobster dinners and brought them back to the hospital room. While I was gone, the nurses helped Melissa get dressed up in her bed. When I returned to the room with the bags of food, it was quite a sight to see her in her new nightgown, wig, and makeup. It had been many months since she had looked so beautiful.

"Wow, Melissa, you sure look nice tonight!"

"Thank you. The nurses helped me get all this on," Melissa said with a little more energy and excitement in her voice.

"Here, I have a gift to help you get even more dressed up," I announced. "You can wear it right now."

"Oh, really, what is it?" Melissa asked, as she opened the wrapping of the thin, rectangular box containing the pearls.

"It's a pearl necklace, Melissa. That's the traditional gift for a thirtieth wedding anniversary."

I placed the pearls around Melissa's neck and read the anniversary card. Before we began to eat our dinner, I called in one of the nurses who had helped Melissa get dressed.

"Thank you so much for going out of your way to help us celebrate our anniversary," I said with great appreciation.

"Oh, sure. It was my pleasure. Melissa is so sweet and she looks wonderful tonight."

"Would you do us one more favor and take a picture of Melissa and me together?"

"Yes, of course, that's a great idea."

I handed the nurse my camera, and Melissa and I posed for a couple of shots. Later, while enjoying our private dinner together, I took a few more pictures of her to mark the occasion. It was a very special celebration, made even more precious by the events that would take place in the coming weeks.

MAKING STEADY IMPROVEMENT

By January 30, Melissa was infection-free, and her wounds were making steady improvement. Unfortunately, the necrotic tissues on her hand and foot were only getting worse, and they were extremely painful to the lightest touch. Despite the necrotic tissues, the doctors, and I'm sure the insurance company, were realizing that Melissa no longer needed daily doctor visits at a long-term-care hospital. It was time for her to transition to a sub-acute health care center.

I understand that the nursing staff must normally keep some distance between themselves and the patients, but I know they had grown so attached to Melissa and her sense of humor. It was an emotional moment for everyone as the paramedics transported Melissa out of her room for the trip to the health care center. Melissa's assigned nurse, at this moment of her departure, was the same one who had been on duty the day Melissa first arrived in early December. I saw the nurse's eyes welling up with tears, as were mine, as we smiled and she said her farewells to Melissa. The nurse and hospital administrator asked us to keep in touch and let them know how Melissa was doing in the coming weeks.

Melissa was now returning to the same health care center where she had spent a couple weeks back in September, recovering from her initial dialysis treatment—the treatment she had put off for so long. It was closer to our home, and we knew most of the staff from her previous visit. Oddly enough, I missed the long-term-care hospital because Melissa had been there for a couple months. Yet this was a step in the right direction, and the staff continued to treat Melissa's wounds and make the adjustments needed to get her to and from her dialysis sessions.

The wound care was still very painful. To alleviate the pressure on her heels, the nurses used some special boots on her lower legs to keep her heels from contacting the bed. The increase of the necrotic tissue on the fingers of Melissa's left hand became more discouraging. She couldn't use that hand to do anything. The doctors said there was nothing else they could do to increase the blood flow to her hand, even if they rendered her fistula unusable forever. Melissa's other complications from diabetes made any attempt for corrective surgery on her left hand unreasonable. The doctor, however, ordered one more ultrasound of Melissa's left arm, and she was transported to the imaging clinic on Monday, February 12.

I arrived at the health care center around dinnertime on February 12, as usual. The nurses told me that Melissa was still at the imaging clinic for her ultrasound test. I expected her back in a few minutes, but ended up waiting about two hours before I saw the ambulance pulling up to the front of the health care center. This had been an exhausting day for Melissa, made worse by the fact she had missed her lunchtime meal. We now had to get some warmed-over food into her body and get her settled back into her room. The next morning was dialysis again.

After dinner, the nurses made their evening rounds for vital signs and discovered Melissa's temperature to be at 102 degrees. The staff kicked into high gear to get several tubes of blood drawn for lab tests, but that became a torturous experience for Melissa due to her poor circulation and low blood pressure. After several attempts, the nurses finally got enough blood to send off to the lab. When Melissa was settled down and falling off to sleep, much later than usual, I went home. I would learn the next day that the lab results confirmed that she again needed antibiotics for infection.

The next night, Melissa and I celebrated our final Valentine's Day Eve together. When I returned home after that visit, I checked my e-mail and read a message from my sister Sue. Earlier that day, she and my nephew had been remembering the anniversary of our sister Pat's home going, twelve years and two days before. They also had realized that the next day, Valentine's Day, would be the twelfth anniversary of Pat's memorial service. As I e-mailed back to Sue, and shared some thoughts about the memory of our sister, I mentioned that the last two days had been very difficult. I closed the brief e-mail message by saying, "I pray tomorrow will be a better day for Melissa."

CHAPTER 11

Setting the Record Straight

As I continued gathering more facts about Melissa's real life story from Melissa, her children, and her sister, I was beginning to sort out fact from the fiction she had previously told me. There were many details I would never know, but I was discovering that some elements of her fictional life had some connection to her real life. Melissa's creativity in crafts apparently extended to her ability to tell a good story. In recent years, when I would occasionally find her talking to herself softly, I'd ask her what she was doing. She would say that she was writing a story in her head—for example, a romance novel. From all that I know now, she may have been trying to write a book about the amazing secret she had kept from me all those years. I encouraged her to get on the computer and start writing a novel, but she never did.

STARTING WITH THE BIRTHPLACE

The fact of Melissa's birthplace is certain. According to her birth certificate, she was born in Kansas City, Missouri, on December 6, 1938, to Charles Lammons and Josephine

Castillo. Although this seemed like a simple fact to begin building on, I still had some questions in my mind. These were not questions about Melissa's truthfulness, but rather questions about whether she even knew the full truth of her birth. Melissa told me that Charles denied being her father when she tracked him down by telephone in the early 1960s. He told her that the last time he saw her mother, Josephine, she was at a party with a bunch of guys. It seemed to me that there were three real possibilities: Charles was the father and was denying it; Charles wasn't the father and was stating the truth; or, Charles was the father and didn't know it.

Charles and Jo had a relationship at the right time for Melissa's birth in 1938, and perhaps that is why Jo provided Charles as the father's name, even if she knew he wasn't the father. Anybody who knew them would have thought that plausible. Even more speculative on my part was the possibility that Melissa wasn't even Josephine's daughter. Josephine's and Charles' physical traits didn't match any of the pictures of Melissa from childhood through adulthood. Only Jo knows these answers for certain, and she is no longer with us.

Melissa claimed that her mother, Josephine, had broken the news to her about being adopted a few weeks before we got married. Her revelation to me about her true background would indicate that the whole conversation with her mother about adoption was fabricated. I wondered, though, if her mother had revealed something new to Melissa regarding Charles Lammons. Was Melissa's story about learning from her mother that she was adopted actually bolstering her deception?

Although Melissa already knew that Reed Branstetter was her stepfather, was her mother Jo telling her that Charles wasn't her father and, more shocking, that Josephine wasn't her mother? Again, more questions with no answers. So whether Charles was Melissa's birth father or not, I now understood where she got the idea to create her fictitious father, "Paul Carrington,"

Charles and Josephine 1937

Josephine and Charlene 1941–42

Charlene 1940s

Charlene 1940s

*Josephine, Reed, Charlene, and Barbara
early 1950s*

*Charlene
High School Graduation
1955*

Jim
McCluer North Hockey 1973

Jim and Melissa
at Pat's wedding 1978

Jim and Melissa
1996

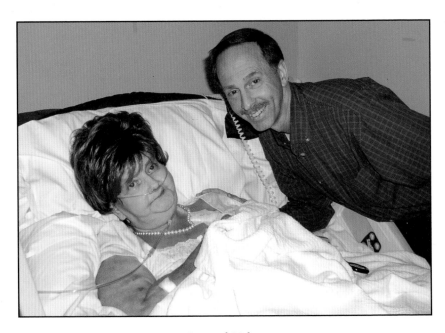

Jim and Melissa
30th Anniversary, January 15, 2007

Melissa's grave marker
2007

as a Navy officer. Barbara's family tree research determined that Charles rose from enlisted rank to Commander or Lieutenant Commander.

When Melissa was four years old, her mother married Reed Branstetter. Her half-sister Barbara came along three years later and both the girls grew up primarily in Kansas City. They also spent time in Los Angeles with Josephine's family while Reed was in Europe during World War II. Melissa became an accomplished pianist as a child, and some of the pictures and documents I found provide record of this fact. In one picture, Barbara is in Charlene's court as Charlene is recognized and crowned the winner of a piano recital.

Melissa had told me early in our marriage that she used to play the piano. For some unexplained reason, she never played for me or anybody else. Perhaps it was too close a tie with her real past and she didn't want to raise any other questions.

Melissa was baptized and confirmed in the Catholic Church, which is consistent with what she had always told me about her childhood. When I asked her where she earned the two dollars shown on her social security statement of earnings in 1953, she said she had served sodas at Panninies Drugstore in Kansas City.

HIGH SCHOOL GRADUATION

Melissa graduated from high school in 1955 at the age of sixteen. One of the pictures I found in the basement shows Barbara sitting in front of a piano with a cat in her hands, a diploma on the piano, and this caption: *Barbara, Whiskers, KC, MO, Charlene's graduation diploma on piano, 1955.*

About this same time, Jo and Reed were getting divorced. Barbara went to live with her dad, while Melissa went to live with Jo and her new husband, Joe Brewer. When Melissa had previously told me about having a job at a drugstore, she had also mentioned that this same drugstore was where her mother, Jo, used to talk to her future husband, Joe, on the telephone. Melissa said Joe had eventually kicked her out of their home on Vivion, and she went to live with a friend named Pauline on Troost. These very precise details Melissa was recalling convinced me that I was hearing the truth. This revelation about her poor relationship with Joe back in 1955–1956 was something that persisted until the late 1970s, when I first met Joe.

Melissa didn't care for Joe as a stepfather, and I had no idea this was based on events of more than twenty years before. Her mother made some attention-grabbing statements about Joe during our final visit to her Kansas City nursing home in 2003. He had passed away a few years before, and Josephine was reminiscing about the days when the three of them lived on Vivion. She talked as if this had occurred many years earlier than the late 1970s, when I believed she and Joe had been married. I was confused by what Josephine was saying, but Melissa attributed the confusion to her mother's dementia. Melissa asked me to humor her mother and not to make a big deal out of it. As I'm sure happened many times throughout our marriage, without my knowledge, Melissa dodged some truth that was spilling out right in front of me.

First Marriage

Only a year after graduating from high school, Melissa was married to Ray in May of 1956. I never learned any details about how she and Ray first met each other. All I know is that they were divorced twelve years later in 1968, after having had three children.

I tried to figure out why Melissa chose Chalmette as her childhood home, and why a family including eleven brothers.

151 ~ Setting the Record Straight

After I learned from family members that Ray's dad was Cajun, I thought this may have given Melissa the initial idea about setting her fictitious childhood in Louisiana. Concerning the brothers, I'm speculating that it may have been Charles Lammons' family who provided the idea for that part of her story.

One of the details Melissa told me after her revelation was that she used to spend summers with her grandma on Charles' side of the family in Topeka, Kansas. She even remembered the street address and the fact that there was a porch swing. This detail raised a question in my mind. If Charles wasn't her birth father, why did Melissa get into a relationship with his mother? Melissa's grandmother's name was Aurelia. A little creative Internet searching uncovered a handwritten 1930 census form listing Aurelia as the mother, Charles as one of the children, and several brothers and sisters. It also showed the birth states of these children as being Alabama and Mississippi, perhaps another reason for Melissa's choice to "grow up" in Louisiana and to give her birthplace as Meridian, Mississippi.

My earlier speculation about Melissa not even being Josephine's daughter is reinforced by the coincidence between Melissa's fictitious birthplace of Meridian and that Charles Lammons' family came from Alabama and Mississippi. Another connection to being from the South and the actual existence of a southern accent in Melissa's voice may have been because Ray's family was from Oklahoma. Melissa spent a significant amount of time with Ray's Aunt Laura and other relatives who lived in that state. I believe it was there in Oklahoma that Melissa must have learned her cooking skills. Barbara had told me that Charlene didn't do any cooking while they were growing up in Kansas City.

Melissa had rattled off some more random statements in the hospital during January, including the fact that she had a brief job at Boeing, but it was not clear if that was before or after she married Ray. She also told a story about riding in a taxicab in Enid, Oklahoma, during a snowstorm. Apparently, the taxicab rolled three times and some strangers helped Melissa get to a nearby house to get cleaned up. Perhaps that truth gave Melissa the idea for her story about rolling her fictitious Corvette, conveniently providing an explanation for her teeth problems, as well as the surgery scar from three C-sections. It turns out, as Melissa explained in the hospital, that her supposed gall bladder surgery scar was actually the result of three C-section deliveries of her children.

DIVORCE

After Ray and Melissa divorced in 1968, she initially took the kids to live with some friends in Grandview, Missouri. This location was right in the Belton and Richards-Gebaur area, where one day she and I would live and attend church. Melissa didn't have sufficient income to provide for the children, so she and Ray worked out an amicable agreement for her and the kids to live in the same house as Ray in Lenexa, Kansas. This is where she stayed, raising the children while maintaining a separate room under Ray's roof for about eight years.

At some point in 1975, a picture of me and some references from my hockey buddy Bob—and perhaps other fellow airmen from Dickie-Goober—made their way to Melissa through her friend, Robbie. That I know is fact. What I don't know is how Melissa got from that point to the two of us falling in love with each other over the phone. From her own writing, I know that she saw my photograph before we talked on the phone for the first time. Even if Robbie did not tell her that I was only nineteen years old, Melissa had to realize I was much younger than she was.

Melissa didn't tell me then that she was divorced with three teenaged children. She knew such information would likely prevent us from ever getting together, and this would have been regardless of her weight problem. I keep wondering if she intended to make up this whole parallel life story from the beginning, so that I would fall in love with her. Was she so desperate to get a husband and get out of her current situation that she would deny the existence of her own children?

What Started All This?

I wanted to believe that this started out differently, perhaps even as a joke between Robbie and Melissa. Maybe Robbie had more to do with trying to help Melissa get a husband than Melissa even knew. For that matter, I don't know if Robbie even knew about Melissa being divorced with three children, although I assumed she did. Before ever seeing my picture, Melissa had no motivation to keep this from her co-workers at Montgomery Ward, although living in the same house as your divorced husband for several years might not be something she would have shared.

Sometimes I think Robbie was up to no good, pushing Melissa into something she didn't want to do. At other times, I visualized Melissa orchestrating all the details herself with Robbie's assistance. These are mysteries that most likely will never be solved, short of finding Robbie herself someday and getting her side of the story.

Concerning the references to Lenny Dawson's wife that provided some credibility to Melissa's supposed rapid weight gain, I have no idea if that story was true. I do find it hard to believe that she or Robbie dreamed this up out of thin air. Although I haven't been able to find anything on the Internet since then, perhaps some contemporary news story back in the

1970s provided a basis for the whole idea. The use of named celebrities convinced me that Melissa was the victim of a medical condition out of her control and not someone trying to deceive her future husband.

Hindsight is 20/20

In retrospect, so many things make sense now. Most likely the fact we didn't have any children, even though we weren't trying hard not to have children, was due to Melissa's age or other medical issues she never revealed to me. When she went through early menopause, we attributed that to some side effect of diabetes, but now I realize it wasn't necessarily "early" at all, given Melissa's true age. I now believe the doctor's report about Melissa having miscarriages was another cover story she invented. Her primary care doctor and she must have discussed the fact she had delivered three children via C-section. Melissa probably feared that any details related to this discussion with her doctor could have made it back to me eventually.

I had a brief conversation with this doctor when she called me after Melissa passed away. She confessed to me that she suspected Melissa was older than fifty-one. She also confirmed that she knew from Melissa and the C-section scar that she'd had three children—but this doctor never knew if I was the father of Melissa's children.

When Melissa and I were living in Rolla, Missouri, in the mid-1980s while I attended school, she had a hair permanent go bad. As a result, her hair turned orange and she had to dye it to get it back to a natural color. Melissa later pointed to this event as the reason she began wearing wigs. She said she was having problems with her hair falling out from this bad perm and that wearing wigs became a necessity. I now wonder, however, if Melissa was having hair problems that some women experience naturally as they get older, and she feared that if this condition were linked to a more advanced age, she would have been found out. I now find myself questioning many things and wonder if she created this bad perm situation on her own as an ultimate demonstration of her creativity.

When Melissa's mother celebrated her ninetieth birthday in 2003, Barbara sent us a small album of pictures from that event. We were unable to attend because I had to work up in Omaha on the day of the celebration. As I look back at those pictures now, I see amazing clues that I didn't even notice the first time I saw them. On a table, along with a picture of Josephine when she was around twenty years old, was a large framed photograph of a man in uniform with two small unframed pictures leaning against this man's photo. One of those unframed pictures appeared to be Barbara as a child, and the other one was a young girl I didn't recognize. I now know this other picture was one of those photos I found in our basement of Charlene as a young girl.

The man in uniform was Reed Branstetter—not Paul Carrington or Joe Brewer, whom I must have believed that picture to be. I was puzzled why Barbara had her own picture included in a birthday celebration for Josephine, but, as usual, I let it go. Some other pictures show Barbara at the grave marker of Julian Castillo, Sr., Josephine's father. I believed, at that time, Barbara was taking those pictures for Melissa's benefit so she could see the gravesite of her "adoptive" maternal grandfather. Now, I understand the truth that Barbara was taking a picture of her grandfather's gravesite as well. It was sad to see from the picture that Julian died in 1938, the year Melissa was born.

When Melissa's mother passed away in 2006, we were unable to attend the funeral due to Melissa's poor health. Barbara sent us a copy of the obituary, which also raised some serious questions in my mind, but I guess by this time in our marriage, I was worn out with questioning everything. As I reread the text now, I am dumbfounded I didn't realize back then that something was wrong. It was fascinating to learn that Josephine had come to Kansas City at the age of six, which explained why, according to Melissa's fabricated life story, her mother came back to that city after her divorce from "Paul Carrington." Previously, I had no idea how she ended up living near us in Kansas City. I also didn't understand how Barbara ended up in Kansas City according to the fictional tale of two sisters separated at birth.

Josephine's obituary also revealed that she had thirteen brothers and sisters—perhaps a more likely source for Melissa's fictitious "eleven brothers." The obituary mentioned Joe Brewer as Jo's husband who preceded her in death. At that time, I correctly reasoned that a divorced husband (Paul Carrington) wouldn't normally be listed in an obituary. This was a logical assumption, because Barbara didn't include her own father, Reed Branstetter, as a husband who preceded Jo in death. What was missing was any reference to Melissa's "eleven brothers," for not even Ray was mentioned.

Something else that should have been a major red flag was that the obituary said Barbara and Charlene were the surviving daughters. Since 1978, I wondered how Barbara had developed such a close relationship with Melissa's mother. Now, I was reading right in front of me that they were both daughters of Josephine. As Melissa had allowed her "niece and nephews" to treat her as their mother, I guess I was thinking Jo had informally "adopted" Barbara as her own daughter, and I had presumed Barbara was maintaining this "untruth" in the obituary.

It would be another two years before Barbara would finally get around to sending me a copy of Josephine's memorial service slideshow. Had I seen that video in the summer of 2006, when Josephine passed away, I would have learned Melissa's secret about five months sooner than I eventually did. This video shows a touching progression of childhood-to-adult pictures of not only Josephine, but also Melissa, Barbara, and their families, including some pictures of Melissa and me. Many of the same pictures that I had found in our basement were included in this video. It would have been quite shocking to view this video at home alone while Melissa was experiencing one of her hospital stays in 2006. I can only imagine how difficult it would have been for me to confront her with this information, without her first volunteering her confession, as she ultimately had done in December 2006.

I know Melissa and I were thankful for Barbara and Brent being so close to Jo geographically and relationally. They and their daughters devoted themselves to helping Josephine through her final years in the nursing home, and later they handled all the details in settling her estate. I just didn't know that this devotion was based on the fact that Barbara was Jo's daughter. Barbara's obvious labor of love enabled me to gloss over the fact I had read things in Jo's obituary that I didn't believe were true.

Faced with all this hindsight, a battle waged in my mind and I blamed myself for allowing this deception to take place. *How could I have been so gullible, so naive to fall for this deception in the first place? How did I allow so many signs along the way to go by unchallenged?*

As incredible as I find this whole story to believe myself, I can only imagine what others around me have thought or will be thinking as the details come to light. I can only pray that my foolishness will be used by God in some way to bring more glory to his kingdom. I also pray he will help me trust others in the future, while giving me spiritual discernment about a person's true motives.

Melissa's Voice

As I am documenting all these facts, or at least my best speculations, I believe it is important to consider Melissa's side of the story in more detail. What was it like for her to live with this deception every day of our lives together for more than thirty years? She was in constant denial of her real history as Charlene, and she had to give up so much to marry me and maintain this double life—but the choice was hers, not mine.

Melissa had many opportunities to reminisce with her sister Barbara on the phone when I wasn't around, but she never could share the true stories of her childhood and family with me. She made good attempts to create some of these events, but it was difficult for me to get a full understanding of even the fabricated life she claimed to have lived before we met. Because our future together was more important than knowing about her childhood, I had focused on looking forward and didn't dwell on the mystery of her past.

I now wonder if it got any easier for Melissa to maintain this deception as the years rolled by during our marriage. On one hand, I think that she transformed into the "Melissa" persona that she had created, and it was second nature to keep the fabricated life story separated from reality. On the other hand, knowing that over the years she was also maintaining her memories of her real life with Barbara or Josephine through frequent telephone calls, Melissa had to constantly switch back and forth between her imaginary story and the truth.

I can only imagine how this had to be a life of turmoil in her soul and spirit. How many times did she think, *I've got to tell Jim today?* I'm sure she regretted her decision to deceive me and the resulting denials of her own children, grandchildren, and great-granddaughter. As each month and year went by, it must have become harder for her to reveal the truth.

Although I do have ample justification to condemn Melissa's actions, I still find it hard to do so when I remember the Melissa I loved and shared my life with for so many years. But the reality is that her initial decision to deceive me was not love at all. It was extremely selfish for Melissa to do what she did. If she truly loved me, she wouldn't have considered starting such a con game. Her greatest fear that kept the deception alive for so many years was that I might leave her. After her confession, I don't recall her ever saying that she feared hurting me with the truth. It would appear that up until the very end, Melissa was still thinking selfishly.

Despite this selfishness, Melissa became a loving wife to me, and a dear, close friend to so many people. As I described in earlier chapters of this book, Melissa had a kind and sharing spirit. We all enjoyed her love of life and sense of humor, and she brought joy to everybody around her. Although it took more than thirty years to confess her deception, I can only hope that the redeeming qualities I witnessed in Melissa were authentically from her heart, and not part of the act.

> Love is patient, love is kind. It does not envy, it does not boast, it is not proud. It is not rude, it is not self-seeking, it is not easily angered, it keeps no record of wrongs. Love does not delight in evil but rejoices with the truth. It always protects, always trusts, always hopes, always perseveres.
> (1 Corinthians 13:4–7)

As I learned later from many of her close friends, Melissa's comments at various times alluded to the mystery lurking in her background. I've heard stories describing how she would be talking about something in her past and then would say, "You don't know the half of it." On other occasions, Melissa made comments as if she was about to reveal some deep, dark secret from her childhood, but then she would quickly change the subject to something else. One of her friends told me of the time Melissa confided in her. This friend said that Melissa feared I would leave her if she were to reveal a secret she was keeping from me, although Melissa never revealed what that secret was to this friend. This friend had no responsibility to make sure Melissa told me the truth, and she was as shocked as anybody to hear the full story. If Melissa had decided to make her revelation at that time, it would have come about ten years earlier in our marriage.

I also learned from her sister Barbara that Melissa had to decline attempted communication from old high school friends or relatives trying to reach her through Barbara. Sadly, Barbara herself was confused about why Melissa didn't want to have an e-mail or phone call from an old friend to renew precious memories. I have no doubt that Melissa was in many ways tormented by her choices throughout our marriage.

CHAPTER 12

Saying Good-bye

I stood in the hospital emergency room on Valentine's Day morning, wondering whether Melissa was already at home with the Lord. Soon I was jarred out of my contemplation with a flurry of activity around me.

"Mr. Marr, we have your wife's room ready upstairs in the intensive care unit. We'll now get her ready to transfer," the nurse informed me.

The staff of several nurses unhooked various bags of fluids from floor stands and hooked them onto portable connections on Melissa's bed. They brought in a heart monitoring device to attach to the end of the bed, and they had to transfer her breathing machine to a portable respirator.

When all these steps were completed, the head nurse announced, "Let's go. Mr. Marr, you can come with us."

I followed along with Melissa's entourage, as instructed. For the moment, my familiarity with the hospital environment, where Melissa and I had spent so much time in recent months, enabled me to retain my composure.

Moving to Intensive Care

The nurses navigated Melissa's bed through various hallways and into the large elevators leading up to the intensive care unit. As they approached the ICU entrance, one of the nurses directed me to a waiting room down the hall where she instructed me to remain until a doctor came to get me. I walked into the waiting room and could see that one family had set up a temporary living area on waiting room chairs, with several pieces of luggage spread around the floor. I imagined they were family members who had come into town to be with an ill or injured relative and they had to sleep in the hospital. I settled into a chair and checked for voice messages on my home phone and work phone to pass the time.

Several minutes later, I saw a doctor in a white coat approaching the waiting room door. I assumed he was coming to find me, so I stood up and introduced myself. "I'm Jim Marr. Are you looking for me?"

At the same time I was asking this question, he returned a puzzled look as if he had the wrong person and said, "I'm looking for Melissa Marr's husband. I was expecting someone older."

Sensing he was confused, I clarified, "Yes, I'm Melissa's husband."

As he looked back at me with that puzzled expression, he said, "Oh, all right, let's go back to her room."

As we walked down the hallway and approached the intensive care unit door, I helped ease his confusion. "We've had this problem before, where someone thought she was older than me. I only learned a few weeks ago myself that Melissa is seventeen years older than I'd thought, so I certainly understand your confusion."

The doctor led me to a chair within the nurses' workstation and we sat down to talk. "Mr. Marr, your wife is in very serious condition," the doctor said as he began to candidly share Melissa's prognosis.

The doctor described the range of treatment that can be used for a person in a coma on a respirator. He explained that in a situation where the amount of time a patient was without oxygen is known and the patient is in good health otherwise, extreme measures can be taken. Such procedures include lowering and raising the body temperature with cooling and heating blankets and other experimental techniques.

"In your wife's case," the doctor continued, "we don't know how long she was without oxygen after her cardiac arrest. Since she has several other medical complications, those extreme measures wouldn't likely yield positive results."

"I understand. I appreciate you explaining all of this to me. What is the usual treatment in her situation?"

"For now, we need to ensure that your wife remains stable so we can perform a comprehensive assessment over the next twenty-four hours. What kind of care do you want us to provide for your wife?"

"From what you told me, I understand that those extreme, experimental procedures would not do any good for Melissa. I do need time to better understand her condition and I'm not putting her under a 'do not resuscitate' order."

"Okay, that's what we'll do. We'll make her as comfortable as we can and I'll talk to you tomorrow after we complete our full assessment."

With that said, the doctor led me into Melissa's room and I had a few minutes alone with her while the staff began performing their evaluation of her current vital signs. Melissa was in a room by herself. When the nursing staff wasn't physically in her room, they could see her through a video feed and they were able to review the medical status readings via remote monitors at their workstation, down the hall. While I had some time with Melissa alone, I was talking to her and praying for

God to give me wisdom. I prayed I would not have to make a decision to remove the respirator. That was something I didn't want to do.

Both Melissa and I had a living will that stated we didn't want to be kept alive on machines for more than seven days, if the medical assessment was that we would not recover. If the only treatment being provided was an intravenous food source, we had chosen to have that continued indefinitely. The nurses came in and out of the room over the next few minutes, adjusting Melissa's equipment and getting her comfortable in her room.

It wasn't long before a nurse arrived with the portable equipment to perform dialysis. Melissa and I had met this nurse before at the long-term-care hospital when he had served his rotation there for her bedside dialysis treatments. The nurse said Melissa's kidney doctor wanted to run dialysis again, even though she'd had dialysis the day before. The intent was to help filter out anything that might impair her ability to fight the infections.

I knew the nurse would be in Melissa's room for about three hours, and this meant I wouldn't be able to make any private phone calls during the treatment. Therefore, I decided this was a good opportunity to go back to the health care center from where Melissa had been transported earlier that morning. If Melissa returned to the health care center in a few days, she would be put into another room. I wanted to pick up her clothes and other items and keep them at home while she was in the hospital. I also needed to return the special boots that had been removed from her legs. Depending on how things turned out over the next few days, I didn't want to think about leaving the hospital later to take care of these tasks.

Return to Where We Last Talked

I drove over to the health care center and returned the boots to the charge nurse. A nurse's assistant went with me to Melissa's room so we could pack up her belongings. It was surreal to walk back into her room, where the night before I had read her a Valentine's Day card. The same room where, only hours before, her heart had stopped beating.

"Barbara, Melissa is in the intensive care unit at the hospital," I said to Melissa's roommate to ease her immediate concern.

"Oh, good. When they took her out of the room this morning, I didn't know if she was going to make it or not," Barbara said with a sense of relief.

"She's on a respirator and in a coma. It's very serious, but she's still with us. I imagine it was frightening to be here in the room this morning when the paramedics arrived."

"It sure was. I couldn't see what was going on around the curtain, but I could tell they were trying to restart her heart and get her breathing. I am so sorry, Jim."

"Were you awake when this first started? How did they find out her heart stopped?" I asked, hoping to learn more about what had happened.

"I do remember that the night nurse came in around 4:00 A.M. and they were talking about her low blood sugar. I think they said it was about thirty."

Melissa's blood sugar was normally supposed to be around a hundred, so a reading of thirty was extremely low. Usually, some juice or cookies would help the blood sugar bounce right back.

Barbara continued to explain. "I could hear them helping Melissa swallow some food or drink to get her blood sugar back up. After that, they left the room for about half an hour. When they came back, they couldn't get her to wake up."

"I'm sorry you had to experience all of that. Thank you for letting me know what it was like for Melissa this morning."

I gathered up all of Melissa's things and thanked Barbara for being such a help while they were roommates.

"I don't know what will happen next, but I hope we will see you again if Melissa can come back here. Good-bye, Barbara."

By the time I got home to drop off Melissa's clothes, the phone was already ringing from the hospital.

"Mr. Marr?" the nurse at the intensive care unit asked.

"Yes, this is Jim, what is it?"

"We were starting Melissa on dialysis, but her blood pressure dropped very low as soon as we got started. We had to remove her from the dialysis machine. Are you coming back to the hospital?"

"Yes, of course. I just had to drop off some of Melissa's things at home, but I'm coming right back to the hospital now."

I dumped all of Melissa's clothes and other items from the health care center on the bed and floor and returned to the hospital immediately. When I got back to the intensive care unit, the nurse was finishing cleaning the dialysis equipment. He explained that Melissa was put on some intravenous medication to boost her blood pressure. The next day, Thursday, the doctor would determine if the pressure was sufficient to sustain dialysis treatment.

SPREADING THE WORD

That afternoon, I began making several phone calls to family and friends, expanding the list of people who knew what was going on and, for a few, giving them an opportunity to come see Melissa in the hospital. I had been keeping family and friends informed of Melissa's health status in recent weeks via an e-mail list. Only a few of them knew the whole story about the deception. One couple that I invited to the hospital was not aware of the whole story, and they were surprised when they arrived at the information desk to ask for Melissa's room number.

"We're here to visit Melissa Marr. Could you tell us what room she's in?" our friends asked the receptionist.

"Well, sir, two persons are listed under that name. Is she in her fifties or sixties?"

Our friends paused a moment to think about it and said, "Well, it should be the one in her fifties; she should be in intensive care."

The receptionist asked an escort to bring our friends up to intensive care to ensure they found the correct person. When they arrived, I explained the entire situation to them for the first time. Later, I stopped by the hospital information desk to make sure that they updated the conflicting records. Because Melissa had been checked into the emergency room earlier in the day with a new insurance card showing an age of sixty-eight, the hospital database now had conflicting information. During all the prior visits in the previous two years, Melissa's records showed her age as seventeen years younger.

Dennis and David were the closest family to Colorado Springs. I told them I would see how things went overnight before I would decide if they should drive down from Rawlins. I talked to Suzan in Ohio, and Melissa's sister Barbara in Kansas City, and they decided to wait and see how Melissa progressed over the next twenty-four hours before deciding what to do. They were wrestling with the same issues I faced when my sister Pat passed away. With limited resources and time, they both tried to decide if they should come up immediately or wait longer to see if her condition changed.

MELISSA, ARE YOU THERE?

As I watched Melissa in her bed, her eyes were closed as the respirator helped her breathe at a steady interval. The rhythmic pumping of the machine and the inhaling and exhaling sounds provided a constant reminder of the gravity of the situation. Each time the respirator breathed for Melissa, her chest rose and it appeared she was taking an additional breath on her own. Periodically, she made movements with her arms that were eerily similar to how she normally moved. She even appeared to hold her painful left hand in the same position across her waist as she had done for the last several weeks.

As the doctors assessed Melissa's condition, they explained that although they looked encouraging, these movements were caused by muscle memory and simple reactions in her brain, and not conscious movement. On that first day, the unconscious movement increased to a point that the doctor provided some medicine to reduce what might have turned into dangerous spasms. Whenever I, or anybody else, was in the room, we included Melissa in our conversations. And the doctors thoughtfully took me out into the hallway for conversations that they did not want Melissa to hear.

At various times during the day, when I was alone in Melissa's room, I would begin to cry as I watched her lying helpless in the bed. Words cannot adequately describe what I was feeling as I would be transported in my mind to some precious memory we shared together—and then I would be snapped back to the reality of the moment.

When nighttime came, I stretched out on a couple chairs in Melissa's room and thought I would sleep there in the hospital. After a while, though, I decided to go home and try to get some reasonable sleep. I knew I would likely face some very important and distressing decisions the next day or so, and I needed to avoid physical and mental exhaustion. That night I did not sleep well at home. When I woke up in the middle of the night, I telephoned the nurses' station to see how Melissa was doing. There was no change, and she was still stable on the respirator. I woke up again early in the morning and arrived back at the hospital about 7:00 A.M. on Thursday.

DOCTOR'S REPORT

When the intensive care unit doctor came by for the first time that morning, he asked me to come out into the hallway to discuss my wife's condition. Based on his assessment and experience with cases like Melissa's, he said it was unlikely that she would come out of this coma at all. If she did, she would likely have extremely serious brain damage. The doctor asked me about her living will.

When I described our living wills to him, he was disappointed to hear that hers included the standard Colorado seven-day clause. I told him that I wasn't necessarily holding to those seven days if I found out that dialysis was no longer an option. He explained in no uncertain terms that I should immediately begin calling any family and friends that I wanted to be there at the hospital with Melissa. I asked the doctor again about the arm movements Melissa was making. He agreed with my request to order a consult from a specialist.

I knew I had to weigh the doctor's information with what God was telling me in my spirit. I continued to pray for divine wisdom as I considered the medical facts I had been given. I did not want to give up on Melissa. I know I had prayed before for God's mercy to take her home, but I did not want her departure to be dependent on my deciding to do or not do something. I called Dennis and David and let them know the situation, and within a short time they were on the road from Rawlins to Colorado Springs.

I continued to make some phone calls and spent time talking with Melissa and praying for direction. Throughout the day, I watched as each blood pressure reading was taken and observed that most of the time her blood pressure was very low or didn't even register at all. The kidney doctor did not attempt dialysis on Thursday and increased the medication to get Melissa's blood pressure higher. He said he would make another evaluation the next morning.

The hospital chaplain came by to visit and we had a comforting conversation. She tried to help me understand that God had already made some decisions for me, as evidenced by Melissa's current situation. I still was praying that I would not need to make the decision to remove the respirator, but I could sense the staff was doing all they could do to ease my mind that I had no other alternatives. I knew that with Dennis and David on their way, I would not be taking any action that day. I also needed to wait and find out if the dialysis would work the next morning.

Using a portable defibrillator testing unit Melissa had been provided for periodic checkups from home, I sent a readout over the telephone to her heart doctor. I wanted to know what the device recorded around 4:30 A.M. the previous morning. The nurse who read the results reported some activity on the defibrillator about that time. However, the kind of cardiac arrest Melissa experienced was not due to the condition for which she had the defibrillator implanted. Therefore, the device was unable to fully sense the problem and provide the help Melissa needed on Valentine's Day morning.

JOINED BY FAMILY

Dennis, Little David, and David and his wife, Tammy, arrived Thursday afternoon. I was glad they were able to be with their mother and me at this critical time. They made it clear that it was my decision about what to do with her respirator, and they said they would support me in whatever decision I made. I received the same support from Barbara and Suzan over the phone. Given the amazing discovery of the previous few weeks, it was especially helpful to have the support of Melissa's children and her sister. Likewise, I received similar words of encouragement from my family in St. Louis as they prayed for Melissa and me.

During the afternoon, a couple of my managers from work stopped by briefly with some flowers and cards. As they saw the severity of Melissa's condition, they were deeply moved and unable to keep a dry eye.

As I watched the monitors and talked with the nurse when she came in to check on Melissa, I asked how her blood sugar was doing. I hadn't recalled anybody checking her blood since she arrived at the intensive care unit. I knew that even without eating, the levels could go up very high. By the nurse's reaction, it appeared she had no intention of testing Melissa's blood anymore. I was a little upset and I made it clear that I wanted all the normal procedures to be followed. She returned to the room shortly to test Melissa's blood and administer the appropriate amount of insulin.

The neurological specialist came by to assess Melissa's brain activity and responsiveness. After his examination, he concurred with the intensive care unit doctor and said that any movement Melissa was making was not conscious movement. Other than low-level brain activity to keep her heart pumping and the breathing reactions to the respirator, he saw no other brain activity.

The doctor offered to order an electrical brain activity test but I quickly said, "No, that won't be necessary."

That night, Dennis, David, Tammy, and David went to a motel to allow me to have some time alone at my house. I wasn't at peace yet about making a decision to remove the respirator, but I was looking to the assessment the next morning about dialysis before I did anything else. If dialysis could no longer be performed, this meant in a matter of hours or days, the toxins would build up in Melissa's system to the point that her heart would stop anyway. It would be three days without dialysis by Friday morning. I knew that if dialysis was not possible, I would not just wait and let her die that way.

At Peace Now to Make a Decision

The next morning, Friday, February 16, I woke up with a sense of peace in my heart about what lay ahead of me that day. When I first arrived at Melissa's room that morning, I was disturbed to see that her eyes were wide open with a blank stare up at the ceiling. The nurse was applying some ointment to Melissa's eyes to keep them moist. Her eyes remained open the entire day. I soon heard from a nurse that dialysis was no longer an option.

I requested that Melissa's kidney doctor stop by the room to deliver that decision to me face-to-face. This was the same doctor who usually was matter-of-fact about Melissa's options and had done his best to convince her to start dialysis much sooner than she did.

"Mr. Marr, Melissa's low blood pressure won't tolerate dialysis anymore," he explained.

"So you won't be trying to connect her to the machine at all?"

"No, I'm sorry. There's no point in attempting dialysis. That's all we can do."

I now had the last piece of information I needed to make my decision. As I was about to walk out of the room with the doctor, he continued with a few unexpected compliments.

"I was very impressed with how close you and Melissa remained through all of her health problems. You really stood by her through everything."

As my eyes began to tear up, I could see that his eyes were slightly tearing up as well.

"Thank you so much for everything you did for Melissa. I appreciate it very much," I said, as the doctor left the room.

For the past several years, Melissa and I had made many office visits to see this doctor and his staff. I know he had been through this kind of situation with many patients before Melissa, but it was comforting that he was aware of how upsetting this was for me and I appreciated seeing that sensitivity in his eyes.

When the intensive care unit doctor came to me Friday morning, he was a little more aggressive in his attempts to lead me to a decision.

"I have a couple more friends I need to call first, but I would like you to explain the process for removing the respirator," I said to the doctor as we stood outside Melissa's room. "I only want to remove the respirator—I don't want to do anything that would hasten her death."

"Absolutely not. We don't do that here. We will not be doing anything that would hasten Melissa's death," the doctor stated emphatically.

He went on to explain that the medicine controlling the spasms and the medicine for her low blood pressure would be stopped first. Next, the defibrillator would be deactivated so that it did not attempt to restart her heart if it began slowing down. This would now be a "do not resuscitate" situation. Finally, the respirator frequency would gradually be lowered every few minutes and Melissa would be allowed to breathe on her own if she could. It would be up to God to determine what would happen at that point.

That afternoon, while Dennis, David, Tammy, and I shared time in the room with Melissa, I decided to call her ex-husband, Ray. I had never talked to Ray before, even when I believed he was Melissa's brother. David, of course, had his dad's phone number handy in his cell phone, so he dialed the number for me. I had a brief, but significant, conversation with Ray. I explained what I was about to do and thanked him for his help in making it easier for me to track down their marriage and divorce certificates. That was it. He thanked me for calling, and I was grateful the Lord had put it on my heart to call him.

I made two final calls to Melissa's friends. One of them came by for a brief visit earlier in the day. Melissa's closest friend, who used to make weekly visits with her young daughter when Melissa was at home, made a final visit by herself to see Melissa later in the afternoon. After that final visit, I walked her out through the intensive care unit doors. My eyes welled up with tears as I knew what I had to do next.

I returned to the nurse at the nurses' station and said, "I'm ready."

TIME TO SAY GOOD-BYE

Within a few minutes, the nurses assembled the staff who would prepare Melissa for the removal of the respirator. The nurse stopped the intravenous medicines and the lab technician disabled the defibrillator. The respiratory nurse came in to perform the initial reduction in the respirator rate at about 4:00 P.M. I was asked if I wanted to keep the heart monitor on, and I said yes, but the nurse turned off the audible alarms that would soon be activating if Melissa's vital signs began to change. I stood close by Melissa's bed where I could reach out and touch her throughout the process.

It soon became clear that many of the reactive breaths Melissa was taking earlier were very shallow breaths insufficient to help her in any way. As the respiratory nurse came back in the room every ten minutes and reduced the breathing rate, Melissa's rate of reactive breaths slowed down. Eventually, her heart rate slowed down as well.

Melissa's involuntary movements had subsided over the last twenty-four hours, but about halfway through this gradual reduction in breathing assistance, her shoulders and her face scrunched up all at once and her eyes closed tightly. Her muscles then relaxed and her eyes remained closed for the remainder of her time on this earth. About twenty to thirty minutes later, her heart stopped beating; it was 4:55 p.m., Friday, February 16, 2007. We knew for certain now that Melissa was at home with the Lord.

MEMORIAL SERVICE PREPARATIONS

God in his infinite wisdom was merciful to Melissa, to me, and to her entire family. Early the next morning I wrote Melissa's obituary. That process reminded me again how merciful God was in making sure she confessed her deception before she left this earth. As I wrote the long list of surviving children, grandchildren, and one great-grandchild, I could only imagine what confusion and hurt feelings there would have been to have me unknowingly draft an obituary that would have included none of these family members. I was able to get Dennis, David, and Tammy to review the draft obituary Saturday morning as we shared breakfast together. I assured them that I would be fine by myself at the house for the next several days, as I made the burial arrangements and planned the memorial service for the following Friday. They traveled back to Rawlins and would return later in the week for the memorial service.

Over the next two days, I met with the funeral home staff to make the burial arrangements and the cemetery staff to select a gravesite. Because it was a three-day weekend for President's Day, I would not be able to meet with our pastor and church staff about the memorial service details until Tuesday. That allowed me more time to work on writing the words that I would ask a friend to read for me at the service, as well as create a slideshow including pictures that a few weeks earlier I had never seen. I also went about selecting the music I wanted played during the slideshow.

After a few days of intensive preparation for the memorial service, I prepared the house for the family and close friends who would be arriving later in the week. This was when I began facing things that had remained untouched since Melissa left the house shortly after Thanksgiving. Pill bottles stood where they were when she left the house, and her oxygen machine remained next to the bed along with her walker. Although the whole house was a reminder of Melissa, I moved these medical reminders to the basement.

I was also busy coordinating with the family for travel plans. Dennis, Little David, David, and Tammy would drive down from Rawlins; Barbara, Brent, and Renee would drive out from Kansas City; my sister Sue and brother-in-law Bob would fly out from St. Louis; and Suzan and her husband Jim would fly out from Ohio. The family arrived Wednesday through Thursday night and we all gathered at my home Thursday evening.

I laid out the cherished box of pictures on the dining room table to allow everyone to sift through all the memories it contained. These pictures generated many comments from each of us about Melissa and the different stories we held dear. We laughed about many things and quizzed each other on our recollection of various events—all dumbfounded by Melissa's success at maintaining her parallel life over so many years. One especially touching moment visibly moved Barbara emotionally, as she examined pictures representing her childhood with Charlene. She shared vivid memories of Charlene's piano skills and talked about some of the favorite songs that Charlene played for hours around the house on the piano. Barbara also helped us understand the context of the piles of pictures Melissa had hidden away for such a long time.

The memorial service was held the next morning at Church For All Nations. Only a few close friends knew the story of Melissa's deception. Those friends and the family would be together for a meal after the service and be invited to a brief viewing at the funeral home, before going to the burial at the gravesite. I didn't want to be explaining everything to a large crowd of friends at the memorial service. I knew, however, that many local friends and co-workers were already confused by the obituary they had read in the newspaper. They would only be more confused by things that would be said at the memorial service. Therefore, the text I wrote for the memorial service included a brief reference to the secret Melissa had kept for our entire marriage.

FAMILY AND FRIENDS SAY FAREWELL

Pastor Mark, our senior pastor, opened with his initial remarks and read a brief version of Melissa's obituary. My close friend delivered his personal remarks, followed by the letter I wrote for Melissa. I knew I wouldn't be able to maintain my composure if I read the letter myself.

Dear Melissa Jo Charlene,

I miss you. As I write this letter to you, there is an emptiness in our house. Although you've been in the hospital since Thanksgiving, it is empty knowing that you are not somewhere looking with expectancy for me to arrive. Yet I know that you are finally without pain and enjoying the presence of our Lord and Savior Jesus Christ. For that I am thankful.

As I was preparing for your memorial service, I found a note I had written to you before we ever met face-to-face. It was that note that I eventually gave to you with your engagement ring. The note was dated February 14, 1976:

> Today is Valentine's Day, 1976. I am writing
> this note for the future. I don't know what
> the future holds for us, and at the time I am
> writing this, our lips have not yet touched. But
> I can say based on my feelings toward you now,
> that if I ever get married, I want it to be you.
> If I have given you this card to read, then you
> know it is true. I love you today, tomorrow, and
> "forevah."

It was out of love that I wrote that note.

It was out of love that you couldn't bring yourself
to risk losing me by telling me the truth about your
past.

It was out of love that just a few weeks ago you
finally told me that your nephews and niece that
I've known for thirty years were actually your children, and for that I am deeply grateful.

It was out of love that I forgave you and assured
you of my commitment to you.

It was out of love that your prayers of recommit-
ment to the Lord were honored.

It is out of love that your children are now here
for you and me as we tell you how much we miss
you and care for you.

You have been the love of my life and my closest
friend—only the Lord will be able to fill the void
that now remains in my world. Through our thirty
years of marriage you have always been there to
support, comfort, and encourage me in my successes
and my disappointments. You have been there for
your family and friends and were always ready to
help anyone in need. These last couple of years have
been especially trying for your health and happi-
ness, and I only pray we could have done more to
remove the sickness and pain. I couldn't bear to see

you remain here in this condition, yet I can't bear to see you go.

Through your belief in him, the Lord has now taken away the pain and brought you into your everlasting life. We know this separation is just momentary, and one day we will all be reunited. See you soon. I love you!

Forevah and evah, your husband,

Jim

Barbara stood up to read her memories of her dear sister Charlene. She talked about their experiences growing up together. The part that touched me the most was when Barbara remembered their apartment in Kansas City:

> We had great times there. I remember every time I turned around hearing Charlene say, "I'm the boss of you when Mother and Daddy aren't here"—and she was! I truly admired Charlene in school. She would receive straight A's without opening a book! She was an accomplished pianist in grade school. I have a picture of her as Queen of the Recital at St. Aloysius Catholic School in Kansas City.

My brother-in-law Bob, representing my family in St. Louis, first read some prepared words from my brother and sister-in-law, Bob and Norma, which included some heartfelt thanks for many things:

> Bob and I have so much to be thankful for because of this woman.
>
> Thank you, Jim, for bringing her into our lives.
>
> Thank you, Melissa, for we know you are watching.

Thank you for being kind,

Thank you for being generous,

Thank you for your love of life.

Thank you for loving us even when we aggravated you.

Thank you, Melissa, for helping us through some rough times.

Thank you, Melissa, for just being you.

Bob next read some thoughts prepared by my mom and dad that included these words about Melissa receiving the ultimate healing:

We constantly prayed for Melissa's healing.

We asked, we praised God, and thanked him for his answer.

Our prayers are not always answered the way we think they will be.

On February 16th, when we got the call from Jim that Melissa's spirit was with Jesus, we knew we had the miracle we had asked for.

Finally, Bob read words of comfort from Sue and him. After sharing some stories about Melissa's hospitality to family and friends over the years, he said that it wasn't just about the food and fellowship she had provided, but it was much more. It was about the giving of one's self.

It's all about forgiveness and making peace with God.

She made peace with her husband, with her extended family, and most importantly, she made peace with Jesus Christ her Savior.

Bob closed with this Scripture that describes our life in heaven: "Never again will they hunger; never again will they thirst. The sun will not beat upon them, nor any scorching heat. For the Lamb at the center of the throne will be their shepherd; he will lead them to springs of living water. And God will wipe away every tear from their eyes" (Rev. 7:16–17).

Pastor Mark presented his message to the ninety or so persons gathered for this memorial to Melissa. His key points were so timely and appropriate for this day. He said each one of us is going to die, and we all need to be prepared. To prepare, we must simply accept Jesus as our Savior. He reminded everyone that Melissa is in heaven and is absolutely healed, and that we can all decide to be with her there someday where there will be no pain: "He will wipe every tear from their eyes. There will be no more death or mourning or crying or pain, for the old order of things has passed away" (Rev. 21:4).

> Never again will they hunger; never again will they thirst. The sun will not beat upon them, nor any scorching heat. For the Lamb at the center of the throne will be their shepherd; he will lead them to springs of living water. And God will wipe away every tear from their eyes. (Revelation 7:16–17)

After Pastor Mark led us all in a prayer, he introduced the slideshow celebrating Melissa's life. I had selected two songs to play during this slideshow. The first song, "Home Free," sung

> He will wipe every tear from their eyes. There will be no more death or mourning or crying or pain, for the old order of things has passed away. (Revelation 21:4)

by Wayne Watson, spoke of the ultimate healing that death represents to the believer. The second song, "I Will Rest in You," sung by Mindy Gledhill, included lyrics about returning to the places we knew as a child and our faith to trust in God.

I had played these songs several times at home the previous few days, as I put together the slideshow. I was hoping that in some way it would desensitize me to the emotion that will forever be associated with this music. As the slides flipped through one by one from Charlene's baby pictures to a final picture of Melissa and me celebrating our thirtieth anniversary in the hospital, it was a deeply emotional memorial.

Although the key message of this memorial service was our joy for Melissa being in heaven, we still were sad and missing her dearly. To end on a slightly lighter tone, I had asked Pastor Mark to introduce "our song." He explained how Melissa used to always tell me that this was our song, and then I would ask, "When did this ever become our song?" Our pastor also remarked that this was a first for our church to have this particular song played. As I have now listened more closely to the words from "Don't Go Breaking My Heart," sung by Elton John and Kiki Dee, I see how this song did apply to us, even more so now that I know the truth Melissa kept to herself.

As Elton John and Kiki Dee sang out, our gathered family and I had the opportunity to greet our friends who attended the memorial service. The family and close friends shared a meal together in the church, before heading over to the funeral home for a brief viewing. Unfortunately, the weather was rapidly changing and high winds were forecast along with some snow or ice. Therefore, Suzan, and Jim, and Barbara, Brent, and Renee started traveling back home as soon as the luncheon was over.

The rest of the family and friends shared the private viewing at the funeral home before going to the cemetery for the burial. Although I knew Melissa was no longer in her earthly body, it gave me a point of contact to see her again and say good-bye one final time while I looked at her face. I placed a few special items in the casket, including her Bible, engagement and wedding rings, a small stuffed dog that Melissa used in the hospital to "eat the bugs," the small red Valentine's Day bear I gave Melissa the last time she talked to me in the health care center, and a rosary that belonged to her mother, Josephine, and brought by her sister Barbara from Kansas City.

At the gravesite, we gathered together around the casket to share our final words. One of our close friends, a Messianic Jew, performed a very touching and symbolic act of placing a stone on the casket as he shared a few words about that stone and Melissa. I later learned that the customary Jewish burial includes putting dirt on the casket after it is lowered into the grave. In the Jewish tradition, the stone is placed on the headstone as a way to let the deceased person's spirit know that someone was there to visit them. On many visits of my own to Melissa's gravesite since the burial service, I've discovered a small stone resting on the grave marker—a comforting message to me that this friend or someone else had visited Melissa's gravesite.

After my brother-in-law closed us in prayer, we watched the casket as it was slowly lowered into the ground. Melissa used to say she didn't care about seeing a view of Pikes Peak when we were buying a house or driving around Colorado Springs. I chose a gravesite, however, that symbolically provides her, and anybody visiting her gravesite, a beautiful view of the mountain peak. We all know that Melissa has a much better view of everything from where she is now.

CHAPTER 13

Living through the Grief

After saying our farewells at the gravesite, Dennis, Little David, David, and Tammy immediately headed back to Rawlins to get home before the bad weather arrived. Sue and Bob departed the following morning on their flight to St. Louis. This allowed me to begin the grieving process in the solitude of the home where Melissa and I had shared the last six years. That first weekend, I sent out thank you cards to those who had helped with the memorial service and had sent flowers. I cleaned up things around the house, as I planned to return to work the following week. After being away from the office for a week and a half, I decided it was best to get through that initial return to work sooner rather than later. This would enable me to restore some normality for the long road ahead.

THE INITIAL GRIEF

Although being at home was comforting, it also was a constant reminder of the last few years of Melissa's health problems. I knew she was now enjoying the pleasures of heaven, but it was very hard to keep my memories from returning to the pain she had endured. Those sad memories initially triggered tears on a daily basis, as well as other moments when I would suddenly remember that Melissa was gone. She would always joke about how much facial tissue the Marr family used around the house. Well, I was probably using double or triple my usual quota during those initial days and weeks after the memorial service.

Anytime the phone rang from an outside line those first few days back at work, I immediately thought it was Melissa trying to call me. If I had to work later than usual at the office, my first thought was to call home to let her know. Some days, after keeping busy at work, the emotions didn't hit me until I returned home and opened the door.

One day, I was getting some exercise in the basement by hitting a tennis ball against the wall, as I used to do many months before, when Melissa was at home. When I accidentally hit the furnace ductwork with a loud crashing bang, I immediately began yelling upstairs to Melissa to say I was sorry for the noise. She was not there. Another day, I went to get something out of the cabinet and saw a box of fruit rollups that she loved to have for a snack. I cried. I cherished these moments when they occurred, and I began feeling guilty when I made it through an entire day without such an event. To move forward into what God destined for the rest of my life, I knew these moments would have to grow less frequent.

GIVING AWAY MEMORIES

Remembering the instructions Melissa provided me in January, I made it a high priority in those first few weeks to give some of her possessions to family and friends. I viewed that as a key task that had to be done before I tackled other things around the house. Most of the items were special groups of baskets within her Longaberger baskets collection that weren't even on display in the house. Instead, they were stored away in bags and boxes in the basement. I painstakingly looked up the baskets in a collector's guide to ensure I was sending the correct set of baskets to each family member Melissa had named. In addition to the baskets, she had her prized collection of quilting material and other sewing supplies. I made sure those were properly distributed to some of her family members and friends who shared her passion for crafts and quilting.

While making trip after trip to the post office, I realized Melissa's daughter might like to have some of her clothes. This desire to complete all of the shipments out of the house right away led me to begin the emotional task of going through the closets and drawers much sooner than I had expected. It brought back many good memories as I recalled times when Melissa wore a particular item of clothing.

As I carefully checked each pocket, I occasionally encountered a ticket stub from a movie we had attended years before, or found an unopened piece of candy that Melissa kept available for her diabetes. Although some friends from church had offered to help me with such tasks, I knew this was something that only I could do in the way I wanted it done. I boxed up the items that Suzan could use and put them in the mail. When I got down to the few items of clothes Melissa kept at the health care center for going to outpatient dialysis, and that new nightgown she wore on our thirtieth wedding anniversary, I couldn't part with them yet. I carefully folded these clothes and put them into a bag in the basement, with a reminder note attached, reading *Decide on 13 February 2008.* I prepared several other bags of clothes for donation and discarded the rest.

Getting through the clothes gave me the motivation to make an initial pass through the house to clean out those personal items that I would never give away or keep as mementos. I threw out the baskets and bags of prescription bottles and other leftover medical supplies that could not be given to anybody else. I later decided that I didn't want to sell any of Melissa's durable medical items such as the walkers, lift-chair, ambulatory chair, or elevator chair-lift.

I donated the ambulatory chair to my church. For the other items, I was surprised and blessed to see that within thirty minutes of posting them on a Web site, I was able to match up each item with an appreciative recipient. One person said she had to pick up her grandmother from the hospital that day and could definitely use the rolling walker. Within hours, she was at the house to pick it up. Eventually, I painted over the scrape marks on the walls caused by Melissa's rolling walker, because it had become too upsetting each day to see those reminders. I was trying to have more pleasant thoughts of Melissa in heaven or in better days on earth, rather than the final year or two of her health problems.

FINDING TREASURES FROM THE PAST

As I made the rounds from room to room, I made more surprising discoveries of things Melissa had hidden from me in the house. When I was gathering up the sewing supplies, I checked each bag or box of fabric to ensure I wasn't unknowingly giving away something I might want to keep. In the bottom of one of those boxes I found a folder with about a dozen sheets of piano music. Written on many of the sheets of music in Melissa's handwriting, was the name "Charlene Branstetter." It was incredible to hold these sheets in my hand and realize that Melissa had played piano from them several years before I was even born. *Nola* and *Glow-worm*—two of Melissa's favorites that Barbara told us about the night before the memorial service—were included in this collection.

The next even more amazing discovery I made in the house was a copy of a letter originally written from Reed Branstetter to his wife Josephine from Germany, on April 29, 1945. I found a copy of this letter on April 23, 2007 in a quilt cabinet in our living room. Barbara later told me that she had mailed that copy to Melissa sometime in 2006.

One day back in October or November of 2006, I had come home to find Melissa stranded by the quilt cabinet. She said she was trying to find some of her fall decorations. Fortunately, she had not fallen down. She was able to get seated on the chair of her rolling walker with no strength remaining to get back up. The phone was out of reach again, so she had to wait for me to come home. Fortunately, no paramedics were needed that time.

After finding this World War II era letter under some quilts in April and remembering that episode when Melissa was stranded at the quilt cabinet, I wondered if she had been trying to hide the letter at that time—or perhaps she was trying to retrieve it from where she had placed it months before. It was touching to me to read this letter from a father to his wife talking about his two girls—including his own censorship as written in the letter:

April-29-45

Germany

My Darling Wife

How are you and the children getting along? OK I hope, I am OK, but how I wish I was there with you and the children. It seems like I have been gone a lifetime. Well, Honey, from what I see in the paper over here, it doesn't look like I will get out very soon. Only men over 42 years of age and men with four or five years service have a chance and maybe all of the d_____ wars will end someday at least I hope so.

Darling, in your last letter you were taking Charlene to the doctor. Does he think she will be alright? I sure hope so. Tell Charlene I received her letter. She can write good. Do you have to help her spell the words?

I can just see her now trying to write a letter. Ha! Bet she talks all the time huh? Give her a big hug and kiss for me.

How is Barbara Joy? Just think she is almost a year old she will be walking before long and into everything ha! Give her a big hug and kiss for me.

Darling how are you feeling? Miss me huh? You better. I was talking to Red yesterday, told him what you said about the mustache. Also told him he had better shave that brush off ha! Red said to tell all of you hello.

Honey, I am sending you another picture of a German town we came thru. It isn't torn up much. You can see the white flags hanging from the windows.

Darling, it is time for me to go to bed, so take good care of yourself and the children, remember love only you, and am lonesome as h_____. Tell everyone hello and answer real soon.

All My Love

Your Loving Husband

Reed

P.S.

I will try and send you a picture of me soon.

Around the same time I found this letter, I stumbled onto a couple more treasures from Melissa's past. The first was a *Raggedy Ann in Cookie Land* book. Melissa had a collection of Raggedy Ann and Andy books and dolls she had bought or made over the years. When I was deciding which of those items I might give as birthday presents to the daughter of Melissa's best friend, as well as Melissa's great-granddaughter, I took a close look at one of the older books.

Melissa had picked up most of these books at garage sales, but one particular book was one she'd owned as a child. Apparently, I never looked at it very closely before. As I opened the first few pages, I saw in childlike handwriting, "Charlene." On another page, I read, "Charlene Branstetter" with a street address on Bales. I later learned from Barbara that Bales was the street where their grandmother lived. Apparently, this was Melissa's childhood book from the time before Josephine married Barbara's father, Reed, and when Jo was living with her mother on Bales street in Kansas City. The copyright date on this book was 1931, so it could have been in the family for several years before Melissa was born.

Finding this old book caused me to run through the house to check several other old hardbacks Melissa had on display from garage sales. Most of them showed no signs of being anything from Melissa's childhood, except for a copy of *Little Women*, by Louisa May Alcott. Melissa used to tell me that this classic novel was one of her favorites as a child, so I had new motivation to scan every page for any evidence of her past.

At first, I couldn't find any writing in the book at all. Then I examined the inside cover and I realized the dark-blue ink in the upper-left corner was covering some handwriting. By holding the book up to the light at various angles, I started to recognize a few letters, and then, a few words. "To Charlene" started off the inscription, and I could see the word "Daddy" at the end. It was dated December 6, 1948—Melissa's tenth birthday. Once again, I was reminded how sad it was that Melissa's own dysfunctions forced her to deny such treasures in her own memories and in her own house, to protect her secret. I hope someday to figure out a way to extract the entire inscription of this very special birthday gift, given to Melissa as a young child.

Many weeks later, I discovered another item in the basement that contradicted my earlier belief that none of our love notes from the early days remained. Melissa had hidden away one note I wrote to her long ago in 1978, when we had been married a year and a half. As I read my own words written from Keesler Air Force Base, the final sentence took on dramatic meaning in light of all Melissa and I experienced since I wrote the note. Throughout our entire marriage, Melissa lived with the fear that someday I might discover the truth of her past and decide to leave her. Perhaps that is why she chose to preserve this one note in particular, probably as a sort of insurance policy for her own heart. I thank God that he was faithful to keep us together for the twenty-nine years that followed:

Mon 19 Jun 1978 525 pm

Hi Baby,

I love you, Sugah. I have to work on my speech tonight so just a few words. I need to hold you and kiss you Baby! I miss you Baby! I miss you very much and it sure was nice to talk to you at length this weekend. Take good care of yourself.

Nevah evah will I evah leave you Melissa. Love, Jim

P.S. Here are some stamps.

CHAPTER 14

Fulfilling
God's Purpose

During the initial weeks of grieving, I decided to get away from the house and go ice skating. With so much of my connection to Melissa involving skating—my initial meeting with Melissa through a fellow hockey player, my first realization that I loved Melissa occurring in a skating rink, and the hours we spent watching figure skating on television or in person—it seemed logical that this was an important step in my recovery. I would have gone to the Air Force Academy rink that was closest to my house, but it wasn't open that day. So instead, I went to the skating rink in Memorial Park, near downtown Colorado Springs. This act of ice skating became quite emotional.

En route to the skating rink I passed several locations where Melissa and I traveled many times to her heart doctor, retina doctor, outpatient surgery clinic, kidney doctor, and dialysis center. The rink itself was located a couple blocks south of the hospital where Melissa passed away, across the street from her vascular surgeon's office, a few blocks east of the long-term-care hospital, and a couple miles west of the cemetery where she was buried.

As I took to the ice for the first time in about a year, I was reliving many memories of my life and especially those events when I first met Melissa in 1976. I had similar, but more recent, emotions when I made it back to the Air Force Academy ice rink, a couple months later, and remembered my days as an instructor. Melissa and I attended many cadet hockey games in that rink, and one night she won the drawing for a free Air Force Academy sweatshirt—that very sweatshirt was one I had packed up and sent to her daughter a short time before.

WITH THIS RING

A couple months after Melissa passed away, I performed a simple but profound act as I sat at my kitchen table eating breakfast. I moved my wedding band from my left hand to my right hand. I had no family traditions to follow regarding how a widower wears a wedding band, and I had assumed I would continue to wear mine on my left hand for much longer. But the previous day at work, I was in a casual conversation with someone who didn't know my wife or that she had passed away. He made some simple reference to me being married after glancing at my left hand.

At that moment I knew I wanted to avoid situations where I might have to explain that my wife had passed away. It was hard enough doing that on the phone when someone called for one reason or another asking for Melissa, and usually I felt worse for the other person because I had to drop the sad news on them. God showed me that even in those situations I could share my joy for Melissa being in heaven and use it as an opportunity to be a witness of the faith within me. Wearing my ring on the right hand continued to serve as a reminder of the thirty years of marriage Melissa and I shared together, while avoiding some uncomfortable situations for me and the people around me.

A Hope and A Future

I resumed my involvement in church activities right away, for I knew that was where my strength would come from. I relearned some parts of the media ministry that I hadn't performed in several years, and I began to practice new skills as well. A friend of mine on the media team quickly got me involved in a home fellowship group that provided me regular interaction with a smaller group of people. This helped me gradually adjust to the idea of going anywhere outside of church and work as a widower. It also provided a more intimate setting than the larger church services to share my prayer needs and my progress in dealing with my loss.

As I continued keeping busy with church activities and work, I thought about the purpose of God in my life and how that related to what I had been through the past thirty years with Melissa. I looked to several of my favorite Bible verses for the promise that God has a plan for each of us, and that he's leading us to a sure hope and future, no matter what difficulty we have experienced.

Although the future has hope, I was trying to understand how God's permissive will and perfect will worked in our situation. God could not have condoned the thirty-year deception that Melissa carried out. I find it hard to believe that it was God's

> For I know the plans I have for you, declares the LORD, plans to prosper you and not to harm you, plans to give you hope and a future. (Jeremiah 29:11)

perfect will that I meet and marry Melissa under the circumstances she created. Despite the way we met and fell in love, God's grace was able to bless our lives and enable us to be a blessing to others, and this was true even while Melissa was living a selfish lie throughout our entire marriage. Thankfully, she confessed her sin and received God's forgiveness, as well as mine, before she died. If my decision to marry Melissa is what enabled God to reach into her heart and draw her to him, then it was all worth it.

Although my marriage to Melissa, as it happened, may not have been within the heavenly Father's perfect will, I can see how, in his almighty power, God was able to turn evil to good. As I wrote for her memorial service, Melissa was the "love of my life and my closest friend." In order to achieve any measure of what the world terms success in my Air Force and civilian careers, with the gifts that God had given me, I had to build on one success after another over many years. And through all the years Melissa was there to support me each step of the way—and I do believe this support was out of genuine love. The value of such success in God's terms should only be measured by the opportunities they provide for sharing our faith with others. The apostle Paul had much to boast about in his accomplishments, but he taught us that anything we accomplish in this earth is rubbish compared with the importance of carrying out God's will in our lives.

> I consider everything a loss compared to the surpassing greatness of knowing Christ Jesus my Lord, for whose sake I have lost all things. I consider them rubbish, that I may gain Christ.
> (Philippians 3:8)

As I look forward to my life ahead, I believe the Lord is able to make the end of my days bring even more glory to him and his kingdom than all the years I've lived so far. I know the Lord has a purpose for me that he has known about from before the day I was born. As we make decisions that temporarily divert us from the desired path, he is faithful to fulfill his promise and our purpose if we put our trust in him.

DEALING WITH THE LONELINESS

As God provided me comfort day by day and helped me comprehend the various ways he had been working in my life, I missed

> The Lord will fulfill his purpose for me; your love, O Lord, endures forever—do not abandon the works of your hands.
> (Psalms 138:8)

> It does not, therefore, depend on man's desire or effort, but on God's mercy. For the Scripture says to Pharaoh: I raised you up for this very purpose, that I might display my power in you and that my name might be proclaimed in all the earth.
> (Romans 9:16–17)

Melissa very much. The solitude of my home enabled me to relive the events of our lives together and capture it in writing. But this writing process forced me to deepen my concentration on some extremely emotional events. While some of the emotion was due to sad memories of Melissa's illness, there was also the emotion of missing my best friend, and walking the fine line between solitude and loneliness.

The words I wrote for the memorial service included the statement that. "I couldn't bear to see you remain here in this condition, yet I can't bear to see you go." Now I was torn between two visions of my remaining days on this earth. I couldn't imagine after thirty years of marriage being alone for the rest of my life, but I also couldn't imagine being married to anyone but Melissa.

> He who finds a wife finds what is good and receives favor from the LORD.
> (Proverbs 18:22)

Despite the way in which she and I fell in love with each other, God was faithful to his promises to provide favor for that man who finds a wife.

As I find myself unmarried years later, I know that the Lord has a special purpose and blessing for one who can devote his interests fully to the Lord's purposes. A married man must devote himself to his family along with serving God, and rightfully so. An unmarried man can devote himself to some special calling the Lord may place on his life.

> I would like you to be free from concern. An unmarried man is concerned about the Lord's affairs—how he can please the Lord. But a married man is concerned about the affairs of this world—how he can please his wife—and his interests are divided.
> (1 Corinthians 7:32–34)
>
> Now for the matters you wrote about: It is good for a man not to marry.
> (1 Corinthians 7:1)

Whether or not the Lord will ever lead me to remarry, I can stand on the Scripture that encourages us to be content in our current circumstances. Not that we can't seek God's will in changing our situation, but that we should focus on serving God to the best of our ability right where we find ourselves.

The Lord's faithfulness was helping me through the grieving process, and I became very focused on capturing this story in book form as soon as I could. I began to view this work as a major part of my immediate purpose in life. I felt that documenting these experiences for others to read would demonstrate God's amazing wisdom and mercy in sending his Son Jesus Christ to bring life to all who believe.

> I am not saying this because I am in need, for I have learned to be content whatever the circumstances. I know what it is to be in need, and I know what it is to have plenty. I have learned the secret of being content in any and every situation, whether well fed or hungry, whether living in plenty or in want. I can do everything through him who gives me strength. (Philippians 4:11–13)

ANOTHER CHALLENGE TO MY FAITH

When I believed, with God's help, that I was making significant progress in dealing with my loss, I encountered another

> The thief comes only to steal and kill and destroy; I have come that they may have life, and have it to the full. (John 10:10)

challenge to my faith. My blood test results from a routine physical showed that my prostate specific antigen had increased rapidly since my previous physical about a year and a half before. Although the blood test was within normal range, my family history of prostate cancer influenced the doctor to immediately recommend a biopsy.

As I awaited the biopsy appointment a few weeks later, I was motivated to begin daily confession of the truth of God's Word concerning my healing. My dad had sent Melissa a list of such Scriptures that he used during his battle with prostate cancer and other health issues. Melissa never was motivated to confess these Scriptures for herself, but I should have done more to encourage her to do so. As I battled the guilt of giving up on Melissa's healing in this life, I knew I could only move forward with what the Lord was leading me to do now.

When Melissa and I were first married, we wrestled with questions on faith teaching and walking in divine health. Is it because of a lack of faith that some people are not healed? Although I firmly believed the Scriptures regarding the origination of sickness being from Satan and not from God, God is allowing such events to occur in many lives. I tested my faith in those early years with a simple headache, but later I began to put more faith in physicians and medicine. God has provided us with many medical wonders, and he is the provider of healing in any form, but I still believed it was not God's best.

> He himself bore our sins in his body on the tree, so that we might die to sins and live for righteousness; by his wounds you have been healed.
> (1 Peter 2:24)

The reality was that I accepted such minor

sicknesses as normal, and, of course, I had been dealing with chronic, but infrequent, migraine headaches all my life. I know many times I believed for God to heal my migraines, but when the next one came along many months later, I trusted in the reliable medicine that I always carried with me for such a purpose. The Bible is clear that Jesus Christ's death on the cross not only provided forgiveness of our sins but also healing from sickness.

God's healing has already been provided; it is something that occurred in the past through the eyes of faith. Although our eyes of the physical senses may tell us otherwise, our confession of the truth of God's Word is what manifests that healing in our body. The Scripture also acknowledges that a person must recognize when they are sick, so that they can receive prayer for healing.

> Is any one of you sick? He should call the elders of the church to pray over him and anoint him with oil in the name of the Lord. And the prayer offered in faith will make the sick person well; the Lord will raise him up. If he has sinned, he will be forgiven.
> (James 5:14–15)

Throughout thirty-two years as a Christian, I had prayed many times for my own healing and the healing of others around me. Usually, though, I was trusting that this healing would come through the health professions. I didn't expect to change this mindset overnight. After all, it took time to get my head knowledge of salvation into my spirit before I accepted the Lord as my Savior. I now needed to get the truth of God's healing down into my spirit and be led by God's wisdom about seeking help from the physicians.

In the thirty-ninth year of his reign Asa was afflicted with a disease in his feet. Though his disease was severe, even in his illness he did not seek help from the Lord, but only from the physicians.
(2 Chronicles 16:12)

And a woman was there who had been subject to bleeding for twelve years, but no one could heal her. She came up behind him and touched the edge of his cloak, and immediately her bleeding stopped.
(Luke 8:43–44)

On hearing this, Jesus said, "It is not the healthy who need a doctor, but the sick."
(Matthew 9:12)

A few weeks later, I underwent the biopsy and received the diagnosis from my urologist. They found early stages of cancer in my prostate gland. The doctor asked me to come by the office to borrow a book explaining the medical condition and the various treatments that may be employed. It was a few weeks before I would see the doctor again to get his recommendations. At this stage, I was willing to keep talking to the doctors, but I was dealing with several conflicting thoughts.

On one hand, I knew the Bible said I was healed, and I felt that taking any medical treatment was showing a lack of faith. I wanted to turn this over to God with no more discussion of any treatment. On the other hand, I knew that by going through and growing through the physical battle that lay ahead, God would bring glory to himself, and that in itself would be a positive testimony.

Given that the doctors discovered this cancer early, I knew in medical terms alone that it might be ten years or more before I would ever experience any symptoms of the cancer, but no one could say for sure. With this news arriving soon after losing Melissa, ten years sounded like a long time. I realized any feelings of loneliness I was experiencing at that time might be interfering with my ability to make the best decision about anything. This news only made me realize even more how much I missed my wife.

I thought about how wonderful it would be to go to heaven right at that moment. If I had given up on Melissa, why not give up on myself? As soon as I allowed myself to wallow in these moments of self-pity, the Lord was right there to remind me that this was not his perfect will, and that he had much more for me to do in this earth.

> I am torn between the two: I desire to depart and be with Christ, which is better by far; but it is more necessary for you that I remain in the body. (Philippians 1:23–24)

The day arrived for my follow-up visit with the urologist and, not surprisingly, he recommended surgery as the optimal medical treatment in my situation. I soon learned that a good way to have people tell you how young you are, even though you may not feel that way, is to be diagnosed with prostate cancer. The doctor told me that at my young age of fifty-one the surgery to remove the prostate was the most promising cure for this cancer. He recommended I consider the robotic assisted laparoscopy techniques that provided a much quicker recovery.

I shared my mixed emotions with the doctor about trusting God for my healing while being unsure about agreeing to

> Therefore, my dear brothers, stand firm. Let nothing move you. Always give yourselves fully to the work of the Lord, because you know that your labor in the Lord is not in vain.
> (1 Corinthians 15:58)
>
> Trust in the Lord and do good; dwell in the land and enjoy safe pasture. Delight yourself in the Lord and he will give you the desires of your heart. Commit your way to the Lord; trust in him and he will do this: He will make your righteousness shine like the dawn, the justice of your cause like the noonday sun.
> (Psalms 37:3–6)

any medical treatment. As a minimum, I knew I didn't want to go through any surgery for at least several more months. The doctor referred me to one of his younger staff who was skilled in the newer techniques, a procedure that had a two-month backlog. We agreed that I had time to think about my options, although he was not recommending a long-term, watchful-waiting approach, as may have been the case if I was much older.

As I continued to thank God for my healing, I prayed about what God would have me do concerning prostate surgery. No matter what would happen, I knew God's work in my life was a continuing process, and I needed to stand firm in my trust and faith that he would fulfill his purpose in my life.

CHAPTER 15

A Journey into the Past

Melissa's Childhood Hometown

In October 2007, I traveled to Kansas City, Missouri, to visit Melissa's sister Barbara and her family. I also had the opportunity to have lunch with my hockey buddy, Bob, the one whom I credit with leading me to Melissa in the first place. As Barbara, Brent, and I visited the neighborhood where Charlene and Barbara spent their childhood, I felt like I was experiencing some sort of surreal time-travel. I stood where Charlene had stood some fifty to sixty years before.

We had the incredible opportunity to go inside one of the neighboring apartments on Benton Boulevard, after running into the owner who was directing the restoration of the building. Barbara recalled various events of her childhood that took place in those hallways, on the porch, and back in the alley of the apartment building. It was an extremely moving and emotional experience to be right where Charlene lived and played in innocence, before the deception and before we shared our lives together for thirty years.

Those pictures that I have from Melissa's childhood now take on new meaning as I recognize exactly where they were taken. It's hard to believe that I was within a few miles of all these memories when Melissa and I first met, but to maintain her deception about her past, we couldn't share them together.

A COUPLE MORE DISCOVERIES AT HOME

I made a fascinating rediscovery in my house in November of 2007 when I was looking in the china cabinet. I saw a small glass cup about the size of a shot glass with a handle. I had seen this glass on display in our different homes over the years with other family mementos. At the moment I was reaching to pick up this cup, I was trying to remember if it was something from my family or Melissa's family. I knew it had something written on it, so I picked it up to remind myself what the inscription said.

There it was, clearly etched in the red-shaded glass, "Charlene 1940 KC MO." This was Charlene's little glass cup when she was two years old. Obviously Melissa must have provided me some explanation years ago about this cup belonging to an aunt or other family member with the same name "Charlene." Or she might have said she found it at a garage sale and bought it for the coincidence of the name inscribed in the glass. Whatever story she made up to explain this cup, I never once suspected that it had belonged to Melissa herself.

As I finally finished going through every box stored in my basement, I found one additional linkage to Melissa's past. Similar to the little glass cup, this was an item I had seen before but didn't know how significant it might be. The item was a plastic shopping bag that contained some colorful plastic necklaces. I always remembered these necklaces as something Melissa brought home after a visit with her mother. Over the years, it was one of those sentimental family items that one hangs onto. But I just didn't know what sentiment it held for Melissa. As I pulled the bag out of the bottom of a storage box this time, I looked much closer at the contents. I found the plastic necklaces, but also found a little blue pirate's dagger and a small blue soccer ball. Soon I made the connection in my mind to Mardi Gras and New Orleans, having seen such items from Mardi Gras partygoers while I was stationed in Mississippi. In the bottom of the bag, I saw a rolled-up piece of paper, which I unrolled to see that it was Mardi Gras "carnival currency," dated 1974. Although Melissa had made up the story about growing up near New Orleans, I was now finding evidence that there actually was some connection to New Orleans in her past. Was it Charlene who had gone to Mardi Gras in 1974, or someone from Ray's family, or her mother Josephine? There must have been some family significance to these trinkets that we had in storage for so many years. I asked Melissa's children if they remembered any trips involving New Orleans around that time, but none of them could remember anything to shed light on another unsolved mystery.

Cancer Free

On December 17, 2007, I underwent robotic prostatectomy surgery. While at first I wrestled with the idea of going through with the surgery, the rapid recovery usually experienced by patients of the robotic-assisted approach helped make my decision much easier. I still needed to trust God to guide the surgeons performing this delicate procedure, and to help me experience a quick recovery from the surgery.

After a couple nights in the hospital, I spent ten days at home with a catheter and nineteen staples in my lower abdomen to close the five small incisions used by the robotic instruments.

The recovery proved to be fairly easy, and I didn't even need to take any of the pain medications the doctor had prescribed. I quickly adjusted to my temporary regimen while recovering at home by myself.

During the initial few days, I depended on my good neighbors to help me with a few tasks, but soon I was venturing outside to get my own mail, pick up the paper, or put out my trash. The removal of the catheter and all those staples also proved to be easy and pain-free. Thankfully, the pathology report on the removed prostate provided some comforting news. The prostate showed no cancer at the edges, indicating that most likely all the cancer was successfully removed and it hadn't spread anywhere else in my body.

Within three weeks of the surgery, I was back at work, and after a couple more weeks of minimal lifting restrictions, I was resuming media ministry at my church. My first follow-up blood test a few weeks later confirmed that I was indeed cancer free. Now the medical facts lined up with the truth of God's Word concerning my healing provided though Jesus' shed blood on the cross.

REMEMBERING OUR THIRTIETH WEDDING ANNIVERSARY

When January 15, 2008 arrived, I knew it would be filled with many touching memories. Although the same as any other day, I gave it more significance because this was exactly one year since Melissa and I celebrated our thirtieth wedding anniversary at the long-term-care hospital. I worked a normal day at the office and decided to drive down to that long-term-care hospital as a form of contact with our final anniversary celebration. I picked up some fresh roses on the way that I would later place at Melissa's gravesite.

As I arrived at the long-term-care hospital and entered the building, I asked myself, *Why am I doing this?* Undeterred, I kept on going and took the elevator up to the fifth floor. Although it had been almost a year since Melissa left this hospital, it was just like yesterday as the elevator door opened. I felt as if I was going to walk around the corner and down the hall and find Melissa in her hospital bed. The sounds and the smells all came rushing back into my memory. Naturally, my eyes welled up with some tears, but I forced myself to hold back those emotions long enough to fully experience the many flashbacks I was visualizing from the year before.

As I approached the entrance to the hospital cafeteria, I took a brief glance down the hallway to the entrance of the long-term-care unit. As much as I wanted to see some of the staff who were working there the year before, I knew I shouldn't go down the hall and disrupt their important duties as they served their current patients. I kept walking into the cafeteria eating area where only one or two persons were sitting at some tables. I walked over to a table by the window and shared some private moments with my memories.

I gazed upon the beautiful sunset view of Pikes Peak and the Colorado Springs skyline, a view I had appreciated many times from this cafeteria while eating a meal or taking a brief break from a daily visit with Melissa. I knew at that moment that this had to be my final visit to this building. As I continued to work through these sad memories of January and February of 2007, I understood that I would need to reach some closure before I could focus on what God had in store for me during my remaining days on this earth.

Back out into the hallway and one final glance toward the long-term-care unit entrance, and I was soon on the ground floor heading out to the parking lot. As I exited the building, I heard the chiming bells from a nearby church. In all my previous trips to this hospital in 2006 and 2007, I never once heard those bells ringing. As I drove out of the parking lot to go to the cemetery, I couldn't hold back the emotion anymore. I grabbed for the tissue and kept driving, another grieving milestone reached and conquered.

The route to the cemetery took me right past my urologist's office. I was overwhelmed realizing how much had taken place in the previous year—saying good-bye to Melissa, writing a book manuscript, and being diagnosed and healed of prostate cancer through surgery. I thanked God for his strength in helping me be victorious in the midst of all these trials of my faith. I arrived at Melissa's gravesite with enough light remaining to place the fresh roses in the vase on her grave marker. I took a few moments to think of her body under my feet while her spirit was far away in heaven. According to the Bible, one day her decayed body will rise again to meet the Lord upon his return.

As I left the cemetery and drove toward home, I approached one more memory of that thirtieth wedding anniversary. To complete this re-creation of that significant day, I pulled into Red Lobster for a carry-out meal exactly like the one I had eaten the

According to the Lord's own word, we tell you that we who are still alive, who are left till the coming of the Lord, will certainly not precede those who have fallen asleep. For the Lord himself will come down from heaven, with a loud command, with the voice of the archangel and with the trumpet call of God, and the dead in Christ will rise first. After that, we who are still alive and are left will be caught up together with them in the clouds to meet the Lord in the air. And so we will be with the Lord forever. (1 Thessalonians 4:15–17) year before at Melissa's bedside. As I ate at my kitchen table at home, I was visualizing the moments Melissa and I had shared the year before. They were memories I will forever hold dear in my heart. I finished the meal and turned on the television to see another link to so many memories of the previous couple years—a new season of *American Idol*, Melissa's favorite show.

RELIVING THE FINAL DAYS

When February 13, 2008 arrived, I knew what I had to do. After returning home from work, I retrieved that single bag of clothes I had placed in the basement a year before. The bag contained those last few clothing items that Melissa had worn when she went to outpatient dialysis from the health care center—the very clothes she wore when I last spoke to her in her room. The bag also contained the nightgown she wore in the long-term-care hospital on our thirtieth anniversary. I slowly removed each item from the bag, one by one, and the tears began to flow. I buried my face in one item after the other, drying my eyes and breathing in any remaining fragrance on the fabric. I left the clothes on the bed and headed out to the garage to get into the van.

I drove over to the health care center where, one year before, Melissa and I spent our last moments together in conversation on Valentine's Day Eve. I pulled into a parking space facing the front doors and waited a minute as I took a few deep breaths and collected my thoughts. Because it was after 7:00 P.M., I knew the small lobby would be fairly quiet, as the front desk and offices were unoccupied.

As I walked up to the front door and reached out to grasp the handle, I could sense I was breathing more deeply and had a pounding in my chest. In my mind, I was transported back to a year before. I walked into the lobby and sat down facing the glass doors to the outside, with the open entryway into the three intersecting wings of the health care center behind me. A man in a motorized wheelchair had fallen asleep in front of the lobby aquarium, where he had been receiving some visual therapy watching the tropical fish swimming around the tank. Behind me, in the hallway, were three older women in their wheelchairs carrying on casual conversations about the pills they had to take that night, the medical conditions of so-and-so down the hall, and the events of that day. I first sat quietly for a few minutes, gaining my composure to fully appreciate the memories flooding my mind.

The sounds around me became more magnified as I immersed myself in the moment. The bubbling of the pump on the fish tank next to me, the distant conversations of nurses and patients down the hallways, the sound of rhythmic chimes reminding the medical staff that a patient was awaiting their assistance, and the beeping alarms of an intravenous pump in someone's room that had emptied the current dosage of essential fluids. My mind slowly ventured around the corner and down the hallway toward the room where Melissa and I last talked. As my eyes welled up with tears and my vision blurred, I quickly retreated in my mind to the lobby where I sat.

I reached into my attaché case and pulled out a copy of the first chapter of my book manuscript. I slowly read through that chapter to myself, one more time, to relive the moments, as I originally experienced them. When I reached the part where I read my final Valentine's Day card to Melissa, I pulled out the actual card that I had kept displayed on Melissa's bedside table at home for the past year. Although I had read through this chapter many times before in the past several months, it still was comforting to visualize those moments with Melissa, as if they were happening all over again.

These memories will always be special to me as they bring up the emotions of an extremely difficult time in my life. They will also remind me of God's love and the way he strengthens us to learn and grow through these events in our lives. I was reminding myself once again that I would need to stop living in these memories. Instead, I would have to focus on the joy Melissa is experiencing now in heaven, and the tasks I have to complete before I too am transported into eternity.

I heard some nurses talking as they came into the copier room that had an open doorway into the front lobby. One of the voices sounded familiar. I caught a glimpse of this nurse through the reflection in the front door glass, as she walked behind me through the hallway of the health care center. Similar to the feelings I had when I relived our thirtieth wedding anniversary a month before, at the long-term-care hospital, I thought it would be so special to talk with someone who had helped Melissa the previous year. Instead, I decided that this moment was only for God, Melissa, and me.

The man sleeping in his wheelchair suddenly awakened and realized it was time to go back to his room. With the flick of his wrist on the wheelchair controls, he abruptly backed up and was dragging a coffee table with him, causing a loud scraping noise of the table legs on the tile floor. I jumped up to help him navigate around the furniture and get the table back into proper position. After the peace and quietness of the lobby was restored, I thought I should go home, but I didn't want the moment to end.

I regretted not saying or doing more during that final visit with Melissa a year before. All very natural I'm sure. It was time to move on and I knew this final visit to the health care center was only the beginning of my precious memories that I needed to relive over the next few days. I returned home and, with some reluctance, I gathered up Melissa's clothes from the bed and placed them back into the bag. I walked out to the garage and gently placed the bag of clothes in the trash container.

I woke up at 4:00 A.M. to prepare for work on Valentine's Day morning, 2008. Prior to starting my usual routine, I took a peek out the front window to see if it had snowed overnight as forecasted. No, this Valentine's Day it had not snowed as predicted. Thankfully, this first anniversary of Melissa's cardiac arrest was not the same. I couldn't help but look at the clock around 4:45 A.M., as I ate my breakfast. The phone didn't ring. I would have to save my deeper contemplation for later, for I had a busy day of work ahead of me. As I flew through the day with one task after another, I periodically had flashbacks to a year before in the hospital emergency room or the intensive care unit. But the business of this day helped me maintain my focus and avoid those intense memories at work.

I had one final significant event to relive as I marked the end of this first year since Melissa's home going. On February 16, 2008, I drove to the hospital where I spent those emotionally draining three days saying good-bye in 2007. On the way, I stopped to pick up a single rose arrangement in a glass vase, along with a note card upon which I wrote some special words that would be important later.

I knew this route to the hospital all too well. I glanced at certain buildings along the way where Melissa had medical appointments dozens of times through her declining health. My arrival at the hospital parking garage also evoked individual snapshots in my mind of each medical event that brought me to this location over the past few years. Carrying my attaché case in one hand and the rose vase in the other, I walked through the main level hallways of the hospital leading to the elevator that took me up to the intensive care unit floor. It is beyond description, and by now redundant, the flood of audio and visual memories that bombarded my mind from the main door up to the waiting room, where that intensive care unit doctor first came looking for me on February 14, 2007.

I approached the family waiting room that was a few yards from the double doors leading into the neuro-intensive care unit, where Melissa spent her last days on this earth. I glanced at those doors briefly, as they represented the final step I would have to take to end this series of remembrances that I had imposed upon myself. I entered the waiting room about 3:30 P.M. I placed the rose vase on a table next to my chair and sat down to read. As I had done a few nights earlier at the health care center, I read through the selected portions of my book manuscript that took place at this setting. At first, I was more aware of my current surroundings and the one or two persons coming and going from the waiting room. As the room would periodically empty out, I was drawn more deeply into what I was reading. I was transported in my mind to one year earlier, with all the associated rush of emotions.

As 4:00 P.M. came and went, I became more aware of the passage of each minute, remembering the events that took place behind those double doors a year before. When 4:30 P.M. arrived, I remembered that unique moment when Melissa's eyes closed after having been open all day. As 4:55 P.M. approached, the waiting room was empty, and I stood up to stare at the large sweep second hand on the clock. I vividly recalled those last few minutes, as Melissa's heart rate, ever so slowly, reached zero.

It was time. I put away my manuscript, picked up my attaché case, the rose vase and note card, and walked toward the double doors of the intensive care unit. I pressed the button on the wall and the two doors opened simultaneously with a whooshing sound. Naturally, my eyes welled up a bit as I passed through what seemed to be a barrier that I was hesitant to break through. I glanced over to my left and saw the nurses' station where I first had that discussion with the doctor about Melissa's prognosis on Valentine's Day, 2007.

I kept walking to the corner of the nurses' station and made a left turn toward the room where Melissa's heart had beat for the final time. It goes without saying what thoughts were running through my mind. I saw a nurse to my left who was busy on the computer and the phone. I turned around to walk back to the other side of the nurses' station, nearest the double doors I had just passed through. At that moment, another nurse who was standing farther away at the station noticed that I might need some help.

"Sir, may I help you with something?" the nurse asked.

"Yes, would you please take this rose vase? It's for all of the staff here in the intensive care unit. There's a card for you to read. Thank you."

"Sure, thank you."

The nurse immediately began opening the envelope containing the note card. I'm sure she could see I was holding back tears, as I quickly turned and walked away through the double doors. I kept walking swiftly to the elevators, biting my lip in restraint, as I now imagined the nurse reading the note card:

> 2/16/08
>
> ICU Staff,
>
> Thank you for the care you provided my wife last year.
>
> Melissa Jo Charlene
>
> 6 Dec 38–16 Feb 07 (4:55 P.M.)
>
> God Bless You, Jim

I made my way directly to my van in the parking garage and drove away from the hospital. By that time, I felt a sense of release in my spirit. I realized I had a smile on my face as I thought about how, for at least the next shift or two, Melissa Jo Charlene would be remembered and talked about in the intensive care unit of the hospital.

The sun was setting and the weather was pleasant, so I decided to make a brief visit to the cemetery before heading home. I entered the cemetery grounds and slowly drove the winding road leading to Melissa's gravesite. Along the way, the words of a song playing on a Christian radio station registered in my mind. I was listening to a song titled "Crazy" from the group Mercy Me. The song shares the message that it would be crazy to choose this world over eternal life in the presence of God.

Melissa had chosen eternity over this world. At that moment, as I approached her gravesite, it was as if I could hear her telling me in an audible voice, *Jim, I'm fine, I'll see you soon. Do what God wants you to do and enjoy life; you'll be up here in heaven soon enough.*

Epilogue: Finding an Old Friend

During the fifteen months that passed after I marked the first anniversary of Melissa's home going, I experienced an unquenched desire to make contact with Robbie or any other friend who knew Charlene before she created "Melissa." Melissa had managed to keep her family in the dark about her deception, but I wondered how successful she had been in doing the same with her friends and co-workers at Montgomery Ward. Perhaps she was a little more open about what was going on. Finding Robbie was critical to learning how the deception began in the first place, unless Robbie was also deceived in ways that I can't even imagine. From time to time, I'd search for Robbie's full name on the Internet, knowing how unlikely it would be for me to find that name, assuming she had married and taken her husband's last name. I went so far as to hire a private detective—to no avail.

One day, months after giving up on the search for Robbie, I prepared for one of several garage sales I held to eliminate some of the memories of Melissa around my house. I came across a bright orange ceramic pumpkin in my basement and immediately remembered this artwork had been made by a good friend of Melissa's from her days at Montgomery Ward. As I struggled to remember this woman's name, a woman Melissa had talked about so much when we first met, I turned the pumpkin over to reveal her initials. Although I had never met this person, those two letters were all it took to remember her full name. I now had high hopes of finding Carlotta, a woman with a link to Charlene's past. This time, I was more productive in finding many name matches on the Internet. If Carlotta, a single mom when I met Melissa, had remained unmarried all these years, I believed I had a good chance of finding her.

Unfortunately, each potential lead from the Kansas City area ended up in a disconnected or wrong phone number. I just didn't have enough to go on to start calling every Carlotta with the same last name all around the country. I needed some way of knowing which of these matches might be the one I was looking for. That added clue would come almost a year later when I was digging through some old pictures in a photo album at home. I had forgotten that I had a picture of Carlotta and her children from the late seventies. I instinctively turned the photograph over to reveal what I needed to find—her children's names. This new information would help me confirm which of the Internet search results were related to Carlotta. I was finding entries for her children and what appeared to be her grandchildren. It was clear that Carlotta had moved around the country many times in the last thirty years, making it more difficult to get a current phone number.

Despite my continued failure to find Carlotta, I was convinced I had the right person. I decided it was time to go back to that private investigator whom I had hired to find Robbie. This time, I knew this would be an easy fee for him. With all the prep work I had done on my own, I was sure his added searching ability would yield immediate results. Within a day after paying my retainer fee to the private investigator,

I received an e-mail from Carlotta, this long-lost friend of Melissa's from Montgomery Ward.

A few days later, I had the most surreal hour-long phone call with the friend Melissa had spoken so highly of over thirty-two years earlier. I was so thankful that she was kind enough to contact me, and gracious enough to open up her distant, but crystal clear, memories of Charlene. We covered a number of topics as she shared experiences as if they had happened the day before my phone call.

"I remember how I used to visit Charlene at her house on weekends and we would work on some of our craft projects. She would love to paint shirts with beautiful colors and patterns."

"Oh, yeah, I remember when Melissa, ah, Charlene painted a denim shirt for me before we ever met in person. It had this silly redheaded clown on the back and my hockey team colors and my jersey number in the balloons on the front pocket. She also gave my sisters painted shirts for our first Christmas together," I said.

"Yes, well, my son Dennis was so talented at drawing things that Charlene would frequently ask him to draw patterns that she could use to paint those designs on the shirts."

"I imagine your son may have drawn the clown pattern for that shirt that hangs today in my closet. By the way, speaking of Dennis, did you ever meet Charlene's children, Dennis, Suzan, and David?" I asked.

"Yes, I would see them when I was over at their house, but I never saw the children's father."

I filled Carlotta in on just some of the story about what her friend Charlene had done so many years ago. She reacted in disbelief at everything I shared. Carlotta had no idea that Charlene and the kids were living in the same house with their dad—her divorced husband. I knew I was going to ask Carlotta to read my manuscript, so I didn't want to ruin the whole mystery, but I told her enough to help her understand why I was asking these unusual questions.

"Carlotta, what did Charlene tell you about our wedding? Did she explain why you weren't invited?"

"I knew that she was getting married. She told us that the two of you didn't have much money, so it would be a very small wedding with no reception. That's why she didn't invite anyone from work. I certainly understood her situation, and I didn't really think it was anything unusual at the time."

"But we never met, did we?"

"Well, I do remember one time that I saw the two of you together out at Richards-Gebaur. I lived in an apartment building just north of the base. One of my neighbors in a nearby apartment would occasionally take me out to some of the public functions on base. There was one time that I ran into you and Charlene. I recognized you as her husband, since she had shown me your picture at work."

"Oh, really? Perhaps it was an air show or something. So what happened—did she introduce me to you? Did we talk to you?"

"No. It was strange. Charlene was very surprised to see me that day. I said hello to her, but because she acted like she didn't want to introduce us or say anything else, I just kept walking."

"Wow, that was a close call. I wonder if I even saw that happen. If I did, I'm sure I must have asked her afterward who you were, and she somehow got me to believe some story. Can you imagine what would have happened if you and I had started talking and you asked about her kids or something? Her secret would have been uncovered in our first year of marriage."

"Well that surely explains why she was so surprised. You know, I did remember asking her one time about the kids. I wondered if they were living with the two of you. Charlene told me that they'd moved to Wyoming with their dad. So I knew then that their father was still around."

As I marveled at these new details I was hearing from Carlotta, I finally asked her "the question."

"Do you remember someone named Robbie working with you at Montgomery Ward?"

"Well, that name does sound a little familiar. She may have worked on the day shift. After Charlene stopped working the night shift with me, we would only see each other as I was going home in the morning and she was coming in. Perhaps this Robbie was working with her."

In addition to e-mailing Carlotta my manuscript, I e-mailed a picture that Melissa used to tell me was Robbie and a couple of the photographs that I had believed for thirty years were Melissa, before she had gained weight. The next day, I got an e-mail reply that deepened the mystery about Robbie.

"Jim, I recognize the woman Charlene said was Robbie in that picture, but her name wasn't Robbie. I can't remember her name, but I do know that she worked in our department."

This revelation raised more questions in my mind about who this Robbie really was. Perhaps it was an older woman at Montgomery Ward and Melissa needed to have all these friends appear to be her supposed age of nineteen or twenty years old. But then I reminded myself that my hockey buddy Bob had talked to Robbie on the phone and someone else in the dorm at Dickie Goober had supposedly dated Robbie. What Carlotta revealed next in this e-mail really set my head spinning. She told me the name of the woman whose picture I had fallen in love with in 1976.

"She was working there at Montgomery Ward and going to college. She got married in 1978, but I can't remember her married name."

Certainly, I knew for the last couple years that these photographs, which had such a significant impact on my life, were a real person with a name and a life of her own. But for some reason, finally hearing an actual name put a whole new light on these pictures.

"Some of the younger girls in the department would give out pictures and Charlene would always ask for one."

Ask for one? My gosh, she asked for many pictures including wallet photos and that five-by-seven that I eventually destroyed at her request, I thought as I imagined Melissa gathering the props for the deception she would begin perpetrating on me and my family.

That evening, after this incredible e-mail with Charlene's old friend, my first reaction was to begin some more Internet searching. This time, I began looking for a woman whose picture Charlene had used to represent herself for over thirty years. I assumed this woman of the pictures was an innocent victim in all of this; however, she might be able to provide more clues to finding Robbie. After a few simple searches, my mood and my motivation quickly changed. I began having this terrible feeling that by continuing my search, I might bring anguish to this woman's life. I imagined how that contact might go.

"Hi, my name is Jim. I just wanted to let you know that I fell in love with your picture over thirty-four years ago. Did you work with someone named Robbie?"

Creepy is the word that immediately came to my mind. Creepy. I decided to end my searching and I also realized it would be inappropriate to include this woman's picture in my book layout. If she ever read my book, she would certainly recognize Charlene and remember the time they worked together at Montgomery Ward. Only my minimal description of her photographs might lead her to remember her own college-age pictures. If she would be curious enough to ask me about it on her own initiative, then my conscience would be clear.

I decided it was time to move forward from those events of so many years ago and seek what God would do to bring glory to himself through this story. Although I knew that I would be talking about this story time and time again, as I marketed the book, I would be sharing the story with the intent of revealing God's grace and forgiveness. Although I would talk about the past, I would no longer dwell on going back there. Rather, I would focus on the memories of the love Melissa and I shared together.

After a recent church service at Church For All Nations, I noticed an usher pushing an ambulatory chair past me as I left the sanctuary. He was bringing it to someone who needed assistance making it out to the parking lot. I thought, *That chair is just like the one Melissa used to have.* Then I remembered; it was the one she used to have. I had donated Melissa's ambulatory chair to our church many months before. Although for a moment I had visions of pushing Melissa in that chair to doctor appointments, the Lord quickly replaced those distressing thoughts with a more pleasing vision of her presence in heaven with no need for that chair. I was seeing someone else being helped by this chair that used to help Melissa so much. God was turning my mourning into joy.

> Blessed are you who hunger now, for you will be satisfied. Blessed are you who weep now, for you will laugh.
> (Luke 6:21)

GOD'S GIFT

God gave me a gift of loving Melissa for more than thirty years. I pray that as time goes on and I continue to serve the Lord in ways I can't even imagine right now, the Lord will remind

Trust in the LORD with all your heart and lean not on your own understanding; in all your ways acknowledge him, and he will make your paths straight.
(Proverbs 3:5–6)

Therefore go and make disciples of all nations, baptizing them in the name of the Father and of the Son and of the Holy Spirit, and teaching them to obey everything I have commanded you. And surely I am with you always, to the very end of the age.
(Matthew 28:19–20)

me of his gift. I pray my memories of the sickness and the deception will fade and be replaced only with the memories of the joy Melissa and I shared. I also pray the Lord will always remind me that it was out of love that I chose to stand by Melissa, and it was out of love that God provided the way for us—and all believers in his Son Jesus Christ—to share eternity together.

I now pray for you, the reader, that you will also put your trust in God. I pray he will reveal to you his purpose for your life, and enable you to bless others with your unique God-given gifts. Together, we can look forward to that day we will be serving the Lord in his kingdom, "forevah and evah."